VILLAGE WA

IN

BERKSHIRE

—★—

BERKSHIRE FEDERATION
OF WOMEN'S INSTITUTES

COUNTRYSIDE BOOKS
NEWBURY, BERKSHIRE

First published 1993
© Berkshire Federation of Women's Institutes 1993
Updated and Reprinted 1998

All rights reserved.
No reproduction permitted
without the prior permission
of the publishers:

COUNTRYSIDE BOOKS
3 Catherine Road
Newbury, Berkshire

ISBN 1 85306 507 2

Front cover photograph of Dun Mill, near Hungerford
taken by Bill Meadows

Designed by Mon Mohan

Produced through MRM Associates Ltd., Reading
Typeset by Paragon Typesetters, Queensferry
Printed by J. W. Arrowsmith Ltd., Bristol

CONTENTS

Berkshire

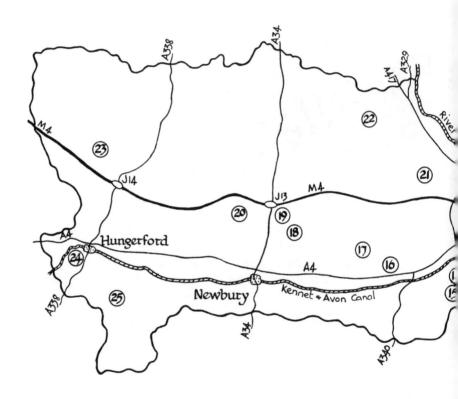

Area map showing location of the walks.

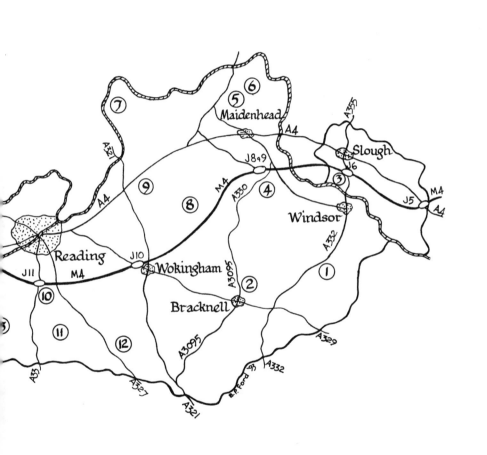

ACKNOWLEDGEMENTS

Berkshire Federation of Women's Institutes would like to thank all the WI members who have supplied the information for these walks. Not only have they given additional descriptive material for the book, but they have re-walked the routes, to ensure they were still available. A list of contributing WIs is given below.

In addition, we would like to thank Brenda Ford for her excellent maps, Judy Fraser for her charming vignettes, and Joyce and Brian Hunt for their help.

We are also grateful to Eva Collinge, Sally Dolphin, Jean Sheppard and Muriel Walker who have assisted by re-walking several of the routes for the latest edition of this book.

LIST OF CONTRIBUTING WIs

Basildon
Boxford
Bucklebury & Marlston
Burchetts Green
Calleva
Cold Ash
Cookham Dean
Cookham Evening
Curridge
Datchet
Eton Wick & Boveney
Finchampstead

Holyport
Hungerford
Lambourn
Mortimer
Padworth
Pound Green, Shinfield
Riseley & Swallowfield
Rosehill
Warfield
Woodford Park
Woolhampton & Midgham

FOREWORD

Royal Berkshire is a beautiful county, from high downland to bird-filled woodland, with the lovely Thames, Kennet, Lambourn and Blackwater rivers and the restored Kennet and Avon Canal providing interest and ideal walking conditions.

It was the infinite variety of the county's villages and countryside which prompted our Sport and Leisure Sub-committee to organise a WI competition for village walks which, in turn, gave rise to this book.

Its original popularity with the public, as well as with W.I. members, has now led to calls for it to be updated and reprinted. This, we and the publishers have been happy to do.

All the walks are circular and have suggestions for car parking. For those who like to break their walk for refreshment the names of, for instance, pubs on or near the route are given. You will find information about the village as well as details of the route and the walks are of varying lengths, making healthy exercise a most enjoyable experience.

The sketch map that accompanies each walk is designed to guide walkers to the starting point and give a simple yet accurate idea of the route to be taken. For those who like the benefit of detailed maps the relevant Ordnance Survey series will be useful. Please remember the Country Code and make sure gates are not left open or any farm animals disturbed.

No special equipment is needed to enjoy the countryside on foot, but do wear a stout pair of shoes and remember that in the height of summer you may encounter lush undergrowth on lesser-walked paths and that at least one muddy patch is likely even on the sunniest day.

We hope that visitors to our county and residents alike will derive much pleasure from this book.

Jean M. Clayton,
Berkshire Federation of
Women's Institutes

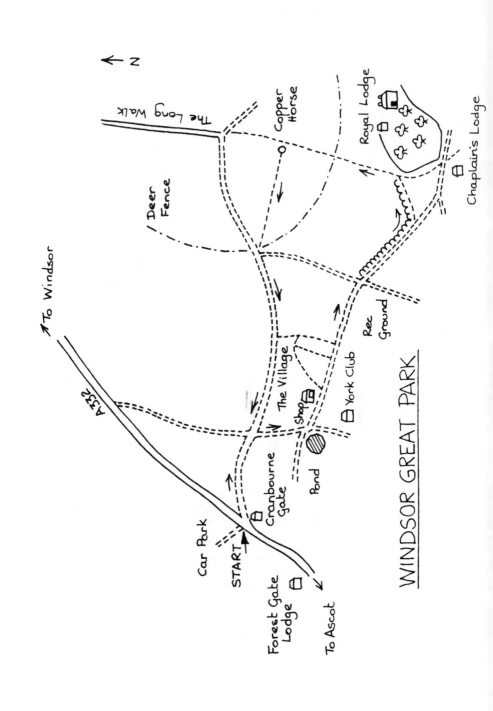

WINDSOR GREAT PARK

1
WINDSOR
GREAT
PARK

★

★ INTRODUCTION: This is an easy and enjoyable walk through some of the quieter and less well known areas of the Great Park, including some superb viewpoints.

Windsor Great Park is probably best known for Savill Gardens, the Valley Gardens and Virginia Water lake, mainly on the Surrey side. The route this walk takes skirts The Village, where park employees live, and the York Club, the hub of village life and sporting activities. A glimpse of Royal Lodge can be seen on the approach to The Copper Horse, the equestrian statue of George III, and the high ground provides distant views over Berks and Bucks.

★ DISTANCE: 3¾ miles. It is suitable for year-round walking. Although the route is partially on park roads, they are very quiet as only permit holders use them, and if you wish to avoid them altogether you can keep to the adjacent parkland.

★ REFRESHMENTS: There are no refreshment facilities on the route apart from purchases from the General Stores. However, there are three pubs on the road to Ascot and on the road to Windsor there are vast areas for those wishing to picnic.

★ HOW TO GET THERE: Approach the Great Park on the A332. Cranbourne Gate is the first gate on the right from

Ascot (just after Forest Gate Lodge) and the second on the left from Windsor. There is car parking opposite.

★ THE WALK: Carefully cross the A332, enter the park through Cranbourne Gate and continue straight on to the crossroads. Turn right and within ¼ mile you will come to Isle of Wight Pond and the York Club on your right and shortly, on your left, the attractive Post Office and General Stores. Note the commemorative stone laid by George VI.

The Village was established in the 1930s, when their Royal Highnesses the Duke (soon to be George VI) and Duchess of York were residing at Royal Lodge. It was designed as a model village, part of the modernisation of the administration of the Estate overseen by the Duke.

Continue with the Village on your left and playing fields on your right. Go straight on at the crossroads and continue to the brow of the hill, Chaplain's Lodge on your right. Turn left on to the track, and go down the hill to the end.

Take the wide, grassed path towards the Copper Horse. Halfway along look right, across the field, for a glimpse of Royal Lodge. You will shortly enter the deer park and arrive at the Copper Horse, the equestrian statue of George III. (It is rumoured the sculptor hanged himself on a nearby tree because he forgot the stirrups!) You are now on Snow Hill, with a lovely view of the Long Walk and Windsor Castle. It is an ideal spot to linger and to consume any refreshments you may have with you.

When you are ready to leave, take the path to the left, by the seat, and after 300 yards, while still on high ground, look right for views over Berks and Bucks. Follow the path, alongside the bridlepath, and after about ¼ mile leave the deer park. (Alternatively, from the Copper Horse go down to the road, turn left and after ½ mile leave the deer park.)

Continue straight on, passing a pond and farm buildings, and return to Cranbourne Gate.

2
WARFIELD

★

★ INTRODUCTION: This is a pleasant country walk with fine views which explores the ancient parish of Warfield, just to the north of Bracknell New Town.

Warfield consists of seven hamlets, loosely linked, for the village has never recovered from its decimation by the Black Death in 1348. Despite the encroachment of development, this is still rural countryside and Warfield has several interesting features, including the church of St Michael and All Angels, built on a Saxon site and parts of which date back to Norman times. Across the churchyard, on the south side, is the parish room, of Tudor origin, which has been sympathetically restored, and close by is Rectory House, once the home of Sir William Herschel, who discovered the planet Uranus.

★ DISTANCE: 5 miles.

★ REFRESHMENTS: Good food may be had at The Cricketers, The Plough and Harrow, and The Three Legged Cross (¼ mile further along the road from the latter).

★ HOW TO GET THERE: From the 'Met Office' roundabout on the north side of Bracknell, take the A3095 Warfield-Maidenhead road. At the crossroads (1½ miles), with The Plough and Harrow on your left, turn right into the Forest Road (B3034). Continue along this road (formerly a drove road), crossing the B3022 (Jigs Lane), and take the third turning left, about ½ mile. This is Cricketers Lane, and The Cricketers pub will be seen a short way along on the left-hand side.

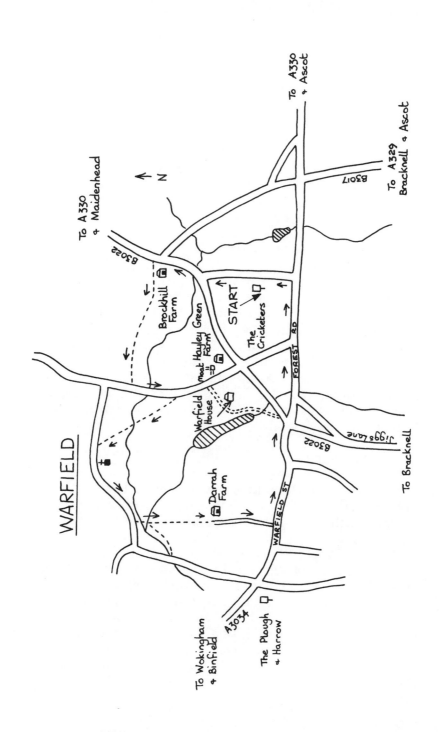

★ THE WALK: From The Cricketers, turn left into Cricketers Lane. Walk to the end of the lane and turn right, then continue along this road, Brock Hill, and pass Brock Hill Farm. Here there is a public footpath sign on the left; take this path across the fields to Malt Hill.

Turn left down Malt Hill and a short distance along the road you will come to another public footpath sign, this time on the right. Take the path which leads across the fields to Church Lane. Turn left at the lane and take the road past the church. St Michael's is worth stopping at to look around. The tower with its recessed timber spire is Perpendicular, and inside in the north chapel there is a 14th century roof and a 15th century screen and rood loft. The restored parish room at one time housed a dame school, but it is now used for Sunday school and church and village functions.

Past the church and Rectory House, once the home of Sir William Herschel, turn left on to another public footpath, at a sharp bend in the road. Proceed along this path across fields to a stile, which marks the end of Gibbins Lane. At the end of the lane, turn left into Warfield Street.

Continue along the road to Fiveways, and thence into Hayley Green. Turn left at the third turning and you are back at Cricketers Lane and The Cricketers public house.

3
ALONG THE THAMES
TO ETON

---★---

★ INTRODUCTION: This is one of the most interesting and beautiful reaches of the river Thames as it flows through the length of Berkshire, passing through Windsor and Eton. The walk combines the peace of the countryside and riverbank with the bustle of intriguing shops and historic buildings.

Eton Wick has managed to retain its rural atmosphere, due in large part to the Common and Lammas lands which the villagers managed to keep as an open space when they were threatened by enclosure in the 19th century. With the support of Eton college, the tithe owners, the then lord of the manor was defeated in 1826, an occasion of great rejoicing in the local community.

What could be more pleasant than to stroll along the towpath from Eton Wick, viewing Windsor Castle across the river and the many interesting examples of flora and fauna along its banks. Then to meander along the main street of Eton itself with its ancient buildings and antiques and art shops filled with enticing treasures. The route passes Eton's oldest building, the Cockpit Inn, established in 1420, and also Eton College, its fine chapel buildings and college houses, founded in 1440 by Henry VI.

★ DISTANCE: 3½ miles with endless opportunities to linger.

★ REFRESHMENTS: Public houses and restaurants along Eton High Street provide plenty of choice for meals or bar snacks, or you can picnic by the river at the Brocas.

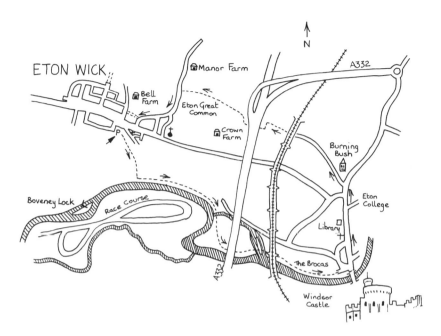

★ HOW TO GET THERE: From the M4 or A4 in Slough join the A3022 to Eton. At the traffic lights at Eton College turn right into the B3026. Follow this road for about 1½ miles to the village of Eton Wick and on the left immediately after the Roman Catholic church and before the village hall enter the free public car park.

★ THE WALK: From the car park walk diagonally across the playing field and along the path to the river. Here turn left and follow the towpath, noting Windsor racecourse across the river and Eton College and Windsor Castle ahead. Birds of all kinds frequent the river banks. You will pass the memorial stone to a college boy killed in a flying accident in 1917, then go over the wooden bridge known locally as the Chinese Bridge.

Here the river winds away from the footpath which takes you under the modern road bridge and railway bridge, noting the brick built viaduct on your left. Proceed into the large open meadow known as the Brocas where you will see many fine swans amongst the pleasure steamers and small craft on

15

the river. Walking next along Brocas Street, the College Boat House is on your right and the Waterman's Arms inn on your left. At the end of the street you will see Windsor Bridge on your right joining Windsor and Eton, but now for foot passengers only.

Turn left and proceed along Eton High Street, noting Kingstable Street on your right, so named as it served as stables for the king's horses and carriages. A little further along on the right see the stocks outside the Cockpit Inn, established in 1420 and Eton's oldest building. There are many antiques shops the length of the street to browse in and many other buildings with interesting histories. The church on your left has now been made into a sanatorium for College boys and a doctor's surgery, with a chapel on the first floor retaining the original east window. The church marks the end of Town End and start of College End.

Proceed over Barnes Pool Bridge into the College environment. At the traffic lights Eton College Chapel is on your right and School Hall and School Library on your left. Outside these is the wrought iron lamp known as the Burning Bush, installed in 1864. Across the road to your right look through the archway into Founder's Yard with its cobbles of Purbeck stone recently renewed from the original quarry. Proceed from the Burning Bush down Common Lane, walking between some of the boys' houses.

Leaving the houses proceed along the footpath through the fields with the M4 to the north and Windsor relief road to the west. Eton Great Common is now fenced to prevent cattle straying on to the busy village roads.

On reaching houses turn left at Brookside and walk towards the village, passing the WI seat donated to the village in 1970, on your left, and a magnificent oak on your right, planted to commemorate Queen Victoria's Diamond Jubilee. Bear left and then turn right on to the main Eton Wick Road and within a few yards you will be back at the village car park.

4
HOLYPORT

─────────────────────────────★─────────────────────────────

★ INTRODUCTION: This walk explores the countryside and farmland around the village of Holyport, an ancient settlement with a pretty village green.

Evidence of Roman roads and settlements has been found around the village, at Moneyrow Green and Stud Green. The village green, just to the north of the route of the walk, is the scene of an annual fair, always held on the first Saturday in June, which attracts visitors from far and wide.

The village has several interesting old properties, including Linden Manor, which was once the home of the Marquis of Milford Haven and was visited regularly by a young Prince Philip before the Second World War, and The Lodge. One of the few Real Tennis courts in the country is to be found here, built in 1889 for The Lodge. This predecessor of lawn tennis originated in the 13th century and the most famous court is that of Henry VIII at Hampton Court.

★ DISTANCE: Approximately 5 miles.

★ REFRESHMENTS: Though there are no obvious places to stop for refreshments, several hostelries are marked on the map.

★ HOW TO GET THERE: Travelling towards Maidenhead on the A330 as one leaves Touchen End turn right on the A3024 towards Windsor. Take the first turning on the left past The Jolly Gardener public house and follow the road along past The White Hart. The Memorial Hall is located on the left just before the tennis courts. This is a reasonable place to park unless there is a function on at the hall.

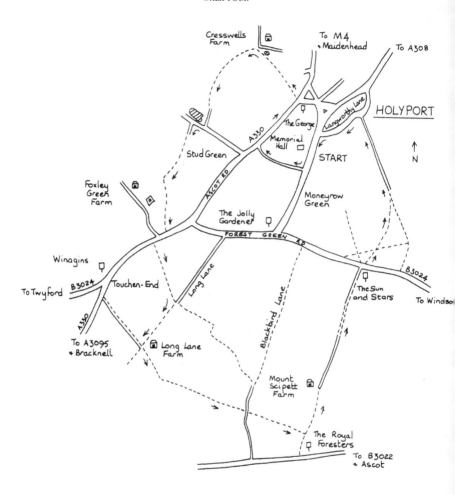

★ THE WALK: From the car park of the Holyport Memorial Hall walk about 100 yards to a right turn into Bartletts Lane. The lane turns into a track and narrows; follow it along to the end where it branches, take the right-hand branch and walk along the marked footpath which follows the busy A330 road. At the end of the path cross the A330 and take the marked footpath over the stile. Go over the second stile and keep to the yellow waymarked path to the gate at the end of the field, by which is a stile.

18

Over the stile, do not follow the left edge of the field to the visible stile but cross the field to the diagonal corner where you meet the corner of a pond (this is Cresswell Farm). Go over the pair of stiles into the field and cross the field diagonally past the sunken area. Climb over the pair of stiles and follow the field edge as it turns left. Go over the stile at the corner and turn right, following the barbed wire fence. At the corner turn left over the broken down stile following the yellow waymarkings. The path becomes a track which meets a road.

Turn right along the road past a pond (Stud Green). Take the marked footpath on the left going along the track. Where the track ends go left over the stile and follow the yellow waymarks. Walk beside the ditch, cross a stile and follow the waymarks along the left edge of the field. Climb over the stile on the left and in the middle of the opposite fence there is another stile; cross the field and climb over this stile. The next stile is at the opposite right-hand corner of the field (this is Foxley Farm). The road which you now meet is the A330, a very busy highway so take care walking along its edge. Walk to the right towards Touchen End.

Cross the road and turn left along the marked footpath. Take the track, turn left and then right following the waymarkings past a conifer hedge. Keep on along the farm track to the barn, and go through the gate where the track meets a public bridleway. Turn right, with the blue waymarks, and walk along the track past the house where there is a footpath to the left clearly marked. Take this path around the garden following the fence and the markings. The path goes beside a fence, then the tree line to the corner of a field; go to the right into the next field (this point was rather overgrown the last time we walked this route).

Follow the yellow arrow painted on the tree along the field edge, turning left and following the ditch to the corner of the big field. Just past this corner the footpath goes to the left over a plank bridge beside a field and over a second plank bridge. Turn right, do not cross the more substantial bridge on the left. Follow the track past the house and take the footpath to the left (yellow waymarks). Go through the gate opposite and cross the field to the stile visible in the middle

19

of the fence. Take care to keep the same direction once over the stile and walk to the tree line on the far side of the next field. Turn left towards the farm buildings and walk up the gentle hill beside the tree line over the plank bridge and stile. (This is Skippett's Farm, spelt 'Scippett' on the OS maps.) Walk along the farm road down the hill. At the end of this road on the right is The Sun and Stars public house.

Opposite the pub there are two footpaths marked. Take the path on the right. Follow the hedge line to the far corner, climb the stile and cross the bridge and keep to the hedge line (yellow waymarks). Over the next bridge and stile keep walking in the same direction (this may seem difficult as four paths cross at this point, your path crosses a field with telephone lines running over it). The footpath crosses the field by the telegraph pole and the stile is by the gate on the far side. Turn left along the track, this is Gay's Lane.

At the end of the lane take the left branch and walk along the country road (Langworthy Lane). At the end of this lane you need only turn left and walk about 50 yards to find the Memorial Hall, but if you wish for a slight detour turn right. You now see Holyport Green on your left, a very pretty village green and on which there is The George public house.

5

COOKHAM AND THE RIVER THAMES

———————————★———————————

★ INTRODUCTION: From Cookham the first part of this walk, from hilltop to riverside, affords superb views of the river Thames and surrounding countryside. Then, strolling along the riverbank the varied bird life, imposing houses and diverse river craft will attract the eye. The optional detour to Odney Weir and Cookham Lock is an attractive walk across National Trust common land, well worth undertaking if time and energy allow.

The famous artist Sir Stanley Spencer was born in Cookham in 1891 and lived and worked here until his death in 1959. A visit to Holy Trinity church will provide a break along the walk and here you can see a copy of Spencer's painting of 'The Last Supper'.

★ DISTANCE: Approximately 3 miles, 4 if the optional walk to Odney Weir and Cookham Lock is undertaken. It is on the whole easy walking, but there are several stiles to negotiate and two short, quite steep, downward inclines.

★ REFRESHMENTS: Picnics can be enjoyed almost anywhere on this walk. In the village there are numerous pubs and smaller eating places where refreshments can be obtained.

★ HOW TO GET THERE: From Cookham High Street, drive across the Moor and turn right into Terry's Lane. After ¼ mile and immediately after passing Poundfield Lane to the left, turn right at the footpath sign. Leave the car in the gravelled parking area.

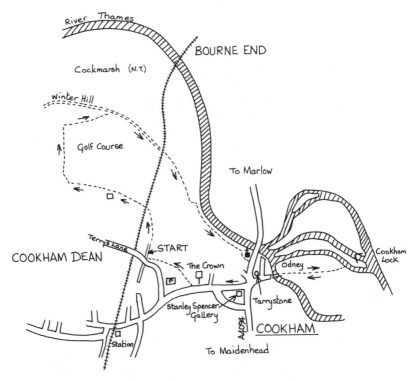

★ THE WALK: Leave the parking area and follow the marked footpath which starts beside the obsolete stile. Proceed to the footbridge across the railway which runs from Cookham to Bourne End. From this path there is a fine view of the river Thames below and to the right. Hedsor church is visible through the trees in the distance. There were settlements here many hundreds of years ago and archaeological 'digs' have unearthed remains and artefacts dating from Roman, Saxon and Norman times. Go over the bridge and watch out for golf balls: the path crosses several fairways of the Winter Hill golf course. Continue uphill on the well-worn path, leaving the clubhouse on your left. Turn right at the top of the incline and take the footpath outside the golf course boundary hedge. This leads to a stile onto Cockmarsh, where there are tumuli of warrior chiefs. Climb over the stile and descend steeply for about 50 yards and before reaching the trees turn right to join a wide path of rabbit-cropped turf.

22

Walk across the rabbit-warren, keeping to the grassy track which, in about 300 yards, becomes a narrow well-defined path. Look out for the raised wooden walkway at the foot of the hill which is used in floodtime. In severe winters this part of the marsh freezes over and is a popular rink for ice-skaters.

In about ¼ mile the path bends left and descends steeply to join the main track skirting the base of Winter Hill. A National Trust sign marks the boundary of Cockmarsh. Turn right over the stile, keep straight ahead for 200 yards and pass beneath the railway line through a short tunnel. Another stile on the right leads on to a broad path. In about a hundred yards turn left over a stile on to the marked 'permitted path' which is bordered on both sides by wild flowers at appropriate times of the year.

In another ¼ mile turn left down the signposted path which quickly brings you to the river bank. Turn right onto the towpath and enjoy the picturesque views both up- and down-stream. Mallards, moorhens, coots and even crested grebes are seen here and of course, the beautiful white swans which nest along the Thames. The swans belong to the Queen or to one or other of the Worshipful Companies of Dyers and Vintners. Cookham Reach is popular with dinghy sailors. Cookham Rag Regatta was revived here in 1988 and takes place annually at the beginning of September.

Continue along the towpath, passing the Sailing Club House (a Civil Service retirement home) to the grassy area where there is mooring for launches and cabin cruisers. Turn right off the towpath just before it reaches Cookham Bridge and pass by the side of a large white house to enter the churchyard and visit Holy Trinity church. There is much to see here: an illustrated guide is available.

Leave the churchyard by the main path through an avenue of yew trees. A small stone erected in memory of Sir Stanley Spencer and his wife Hilda can be found close to the wooden seat on your right. Turn left out of the gate and bear right on to the main Cookham to Bourne End Road and cross it with great care to inspect the Tarrystone on the other side. This large rock of uncertain age has been moved some yards from its original position, where it is recorded on the stone that country sports were held prior to 1507.

23

(An optional diversion can be made here to Odney Island and Weir, and Cookham Lock. Walk down Odney Lane, on the left beyond the Tarrystone. At the end of the lane a bridge across Lullebrook leads to the island and Odney Common. Here cattle graze amidst buttercups and wild parsley in an idyllic setting which can have changed little in several hundred years. Behind them, on the opposite bank, the gardens of the Odney Club stretch to the water's edge. Beyond the common a tarmac path leads to the weir. Before the war there was a bathing place here. Cross the weir bridge by the side gate, and then the bridge in front of you and follow the path round to the right which shortly brings you to peaceful Cookham Lock. From here retrace your steps to the start of Odney Lane and rejoin the main route.)

To continue on the main walk, turn left and in a few yards carefully cross the road to the left-hand corner of the High Street where the Sir Stanley Spencer Gallery, housed in an old Wesleyan chapel, can be visited. (Summer, Easter to end of October inclusive, daily 10.30 am-5.30 pm Winter weekends, Bank Holidays 11 am-5 pm. A small admission fee is payable.) Proceed along the High Street, passing several old inns and Sir Stanley Spencer's birthplace, 'Fernely' (marked wih a plaque). The inn sign of the ancient 'Bel and the Dragon' was painted by Amy Hagerty Spencer, Stanley's cousin. The coaching inn The King's Arms, is now a steakhouse. Beside the Royal Exchange is an attractive arcade of tiny shops.

At the far end of the High Street, on the edge of the Moor, stands The Crown. From outside the pub continue alongside the hedge bordering the Moor, parallel to the road, as far as the large National Trust car park on the left. The built-up causeway and the brick bridge across the Fleet are used when the road across the Moor is flooded. When this happens the path you are walking along and the surrounding fields are under several feet of water.

Continue past the car park in the same direction, follow the footpath sign, cross the stream and stile, and shortly take the left-hand path. Over another stile and a gentle upward slope will bring you back to the small parking area off Terry's Lane where the walk began.

6

COOKHAM DEAN
AND WINTER HILL

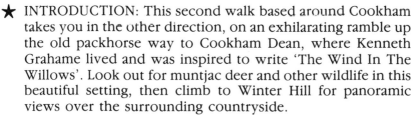

★ INTRODUCTION: This second walk based around Cookham takes you in the other direction, on an exhilarating ramble up the old packhorse way to Cookham Dean, where Kenneth Grahame lived and was inspired to write 'The Wind In The Willows'. Look out for muntjac deer and other wildlife in this beautiful setting, then climb to Winter Hill for panoramic views over the surrounding countryside.

The village of Cookham was an ancient settlement on the banks of the Thames, an important crossing point in the Middle Ages when flocks of sheep were herded from the West Country to London along the 'wool way'. With the building of Maidenhead Bridge, Cookham became a backwater until, with the advent of the railway in the 1850s, Cookham Rise began to develop quite rapidly. In those days Cookham Dean was the wild and lawless area of the three villages, inhabited by gipsies, farm labourers and poachers.

★ DISTANCE: About 4 miles, mainly on footpaths, involving two fairly steep climbs.

★ REFRESHMENTS: Refreshments are available at two pubs in Cookham Dean during licensing hours and there are several suitable picnic sites.

★ HOW TO GET THERE: By train or bus to Cookham station. By car take the B4447 from Maidenhead. At the mini-roundabout by the Old Anchor pub, turn left. Parking is available by the shopping precinct and station.

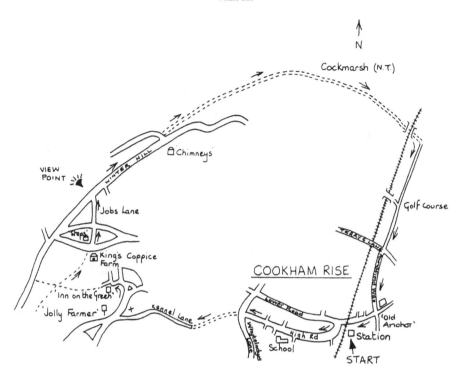

★ THE WALK: From Cookham station cross the level crossing and turn immediately left up High Road. At the top of the hill on the left is Cookham Rise School, the local library and the house in which Sir Stanley Spencer, the famous Cookham painter, spent the last years of his life.

Continue to the junction with Whyteladyes Lane which you cross and take the footpath known as Kennel Lane with the Cricket Club on your right. High Road and Kennel Lane form part of the old 'wool way' – the packhorse route from the sheep country in the west to London, crossing the Thames at a ford at Cookham.

It is a short steep climb to Cookham Dean, where several literary people have lived, including Kenneth Grahame. The countryside and woods inspired him to write The Wind in the Willows. At the top of the hill the footpath joins Church Lane and arrives at the back of St John the Baptist church, built in 1844 to plans by Carpenter. The design was considered so

26

attractive that identical churches were built in Tasmania and Rossmore, New South Wales. Over the weekend nearest to their patronal festival (June 24th) a flower festival is held in the church which is well worth a visit.

Opposite the church is The Jolly Farmer public house where refreshments may be had during licensing hours. Going downhill from the pub, turn left at the war memorial and, skirting the green, at the sign to the Inn on the Green (another source of refreshments) turn left again.

Pass right in front of the pub and take the footpath alongside the pub into a copse. Small muntjac deer, which have become naturalised in this area, can be seen at times, as well as rabbits and the occasional fox. Cross the unusual V-shaped stile and take the footpath straight ahead of you, going downhill and looking towards woods on the opposite slope. When you reach the junction of four footpaths, bear right with the hedge on your left and follow the footpath round the outside of the fenced-off farm buildings. Go through the kissing gate and follow the track to come out on to Kings Lane.

With your back to Old Stables, walk down Kings Lane for about 100 metres until you come to a footpath on the left, next to a house called 'Steps' which climbs quite steeply, crosses Dean Lane and then becomes the byway known as Jobs Lane. At the top of the lane turn right towards Winter Hill, a famous local viewpoint, 225 ft above sea level. Looking north one gets a panoramic view of the river sweeping around the foot of the hill and the attractive Thames-side town of Marlow. In the foreground water-skiers are often in action on the gravel pits. A little further down the road, in the opposite direction, Windsor Castle can be glimpsed between the trees. There are good picnic spots here or further on by Cockmarsh.

Continue down Winter Hill, walking along the road past the junction with Gibraltar Lane, until you see the house on the right called 'Chimneys'. On your left a footpath leaves the road and leads to Cockmarsh. This is a marshy field belonging to the National Trust since 1934. It is a site of scientific interest, having steep chalky slopes to the right, bright in summer with chalk-loving plants and their attendant butterflies. There are Bronze Age burial grounds here. One of the tumuli was excavated in 1874 and the remains of a Saxon

27

warrior found. Ignore the footpath branching off to the left and continue on the footpath at the foot of the hill here, keeping the marshy area, which is often flooded in winter, to your left.

Crossing one more stile, in 200 yards pass under the Maidenhead to Bourne End railway and after climbing a few steps on your right, follow the footpath through the John Lewis Partnership Golf Course. There are picturesque views to the left over Cookham Reach and towards Cliveden. On leaving the golf course continue on the path to Terrys Lane, cross the road and almost immediately opposite take the unmade road, Poundcroft Lane. About half-way down on the left-hand side you will see 'Englefield' where Spencer painted a series of pictures. At the end of Poundcroft Lane turn right up Station Hill back to Cookham station.

7
REMENHAM
AND ASTON
★

★ INTRODUCTION: A delightful walk for any season, the towpath along the banks of the Thames from Remenham to Aston reveals one of the most beautiful stretches of this lovely river. You return by footpath and farm track at a higher level, gaining fine views of the wooded hillsides above the opposite bank.

The horseshoe loop of the Thames between Hurley and Wargrave forms the boundary of the parish of Remenham and provides a variety of scenery and items of interest. The walk begins by the Victorian Gothic church of St Nicholas, constructed on the site of a previous Norman church. This area was once the centre of the old village, until the plague wiped out its heart in the 17th century. Temple Island is not far away along the towpath, the Temple being a Georgian folly at the southern end. The island marks the start of the Henley Royal Regatta course, started in 1839, the 'Henley Reach' running between the Marsh and Hambleden Locks.

Hambleden Lock is a good place to pause for a while, to take the walkway over the weir to watch the canoeists and visit the watermill, which dates back to 1338. Aston was once the landing point for the Hambleden ferry, unfortunately long since abandoned.

★ DISTANCE: An easy 3½ miles of mainly level walking. There is one, not too steep, climb from Aston to reach the higher track on the return route.

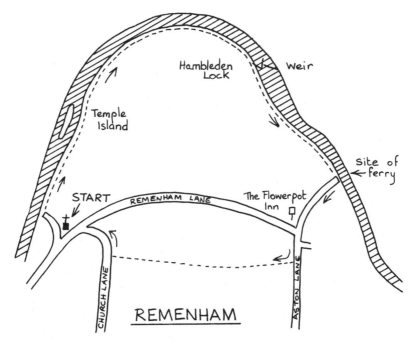

REMENHAM

★ REFRESHMENTS: The Flower Pot Hotel, Aston, at about the halfway mark, provides liquid refreshment and pub lunches.

★ HOW TO GET THERE: Take the A423 Maidenhead-Henley road. Just short of Henley Bridge turn right onto a minor road signposted Remenham. There is limited car parking near the church at Remenham – impossible during Henley Week!

★ THE WALK: Leaving the church on your right, follow a lane, then a track across a stile, to reach the towpath. Here turn right and follow the towpath past Temple Island with its Georgian neo-classical temple. Temple Island is the start of the Henley Royal Regatta Course, which finishes at Henley Bridge. In recent years the island has become the finish of the Ladies' Oxford v Cambridge Boat Race.

Continuing along the towpath, you will have a view across the river of a white Victorian mansion, with beautifully tended grounds and clipped yew hedges – now the Henley Management College. Look out for interesting waterfowl which frequent this stretch of the river. On reaching Hambleden Lock, cross to mid-stream to see the white-boarded Hambleden Mill and excellent views of the river. Returning to the Berkshire bank, the path passes through fields and over a small footbridge to the former site of the Aston ferry. Here turn right up Aston Lane, with banks of many wild flowers during spring and early summer, to reach The Flower Pot. This inn was built in 1890 to cater for oarsmen and anglers in the river's heyday.

After refreshment (if needed!) leave The Flower Pot and continue for a short way up Aston Lane. Do not take the right-hand lane to Remenham. Just after Highway Cottage, turn right and over a stile to follow a climbing path on the right-hand side of a field. At the top of the field, another stile leads to a farm track which returns to Remenham. The track overlooks The Greenlands Estate (the largest single area protected by National Trust Covenants) and donated to the Trust in 1944 by Viscount Hambleden to conserve the Remenham area. The views from this upper track to the wooded slopes above the far bank of the river are particularly fine, especially in late spring and autumn.

When the track reaches a tarmac lane (Church Lane) turn right and continue downhill past cottages with pretty gardens to return to Remenham church.

The church, Victorian and on the site of an older building, may be locked, but the churchyard, which pre-dates it, is worth a visit. Among the headstones is one to Caleb Gould, the lockkeeper at Hambleden who augmented his income by baking bread and selling it to passing bargemen. He died on the 30th May 1836 and his epitaph is unusual and amusing.

31

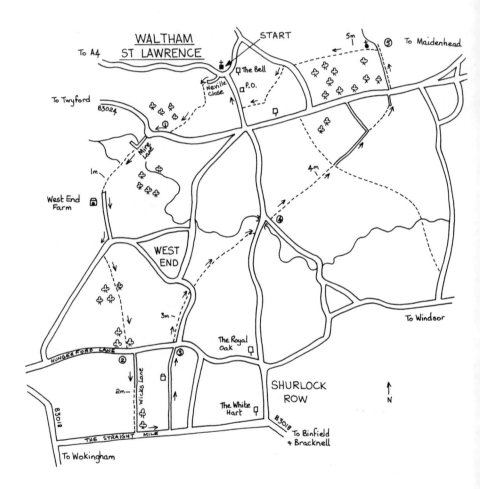

8
WALTHAM
ST LAWRENCE

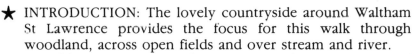

★ INTRODUCTION: The lovely countryside around Waltham St Lawrence provides the focus for this walk through woodland, across open fields and over stream and river.

Waltham St Lawrence has Roman and Saxon roots and artefacts are still occasionally found in the area. The village has a delightful square, with the old pound, the church and a 15th century inn, The Bell, as well as attractive cottages. The pretty church, begun in the 11th century, has had various additions over the years.

Behind the church is Neville Hall, much used by the local community. Like Neville Close, near the beginning of the walk, it is named after a local family who became lords of the manor in 1608. During the Civil War the family was divided, with brothers fighting on opposite sides, and this affected the village, many of the local families supporting the Parliamentarians and the vicar remaining staunchly Royalist.

★ DISTANCE: 6 miles, or 5 miles for the shortened walk.

★ REFRESHMENTS: The Bell inn provides good refreshments.

★ HOW TO GET THERE: From Twyford, just south of the A4, take the B3024 road to Holyport and Maidenhead, passing through Ruscombe. After approximately 3 miles, turn left at the five-way crossroads towards Waltham St Lawrence village centre. The church will be seen ¼ mile ahead. The village can also be reached from the B3018, as seen on the sketch map. Park at the church.

★ THE WALK: With your back to the lychgate, turn right then fork left into Neville Close. At the end of the road take the footpath turning left across a field, then follow the hedge to the right to reach a footbridge and stile. Fork right, passing a large oak tree to a stile in the fence. Cross to a stile in the far left-hand corner of the field. (Point 1)

Cross the road with care into Mire Lane, passing West End Farm after less than ½ mile. At the next road turn right for 100 yards to a footpath sign and stile on the left. Cross the stile and keep alongside the hedge on the left through a 'squeeze-stile' to a further stile leading into a copse. Follow the path to a footbridge on the right and then cross the field past a single oak tree to another footbridge. Go straight ahead, keeping closely to the stream/ditch on the left to pass through the wood to the road. (Point 2) (The walk can be shortened by 1 mile here by walking along the road to Point 3.)

Cross the road diagonally left to Wicks Lane and go straight ahead for ½ mile to the road. Turn left and after 300 yards take the footpath on the left to join a narrow lane at a stile, then passing 'Honeys' to the road. (Point 3)

Cross the road to the footpath and after a footbridge the path joins the lane where it bears left. Shortly turn right before the first house, into a bridleway (*not* the stile and foot-path nearby). The bridleway reaches the road at 'Bent Mead'. Turn left and after crossing the river bridge turn right and quickly left into another bridleway. (Point 4)

Proceed for nearly ¾ mile until the track turns sharp left. At this point take the footpath across the stile, heading for a gate just before the white house on the right. At the road cross diagonally right to take a bridleway through the gates into Shottesbrooke Park, keeping to the right of the copse and heading for the church. (Point 5)

Turn left through the churchyard and walled path, across a stile to a further stile/bridlegate ahead. Follow the edge of the wood to the road. Take the footpath over the stile opposite, heading for a stile on the far side of the field. Follow the white directional arrows over two more stiles and alongside allotments to the road at Paradise Cottage.

Turn right along the road past the village stores and post office, to reach The Bell and the church.

34

9
TWYFORD
LAKES

---★---

★ INTRODUCTION: Twyford is the focal point for this gentle walk across fields and over the river Loddon. The lakes which are such a feature of the walk were all created following gravel extraction in the area and now provide a rich environment for wildlife and wild flowers and grasses.

Twyford, whose name is derived from 'two fords', is a thriving village, which with recent development is now almost the size of a town. However, its High Street, part of the original Bath Road, retains a village atmosphere. In 1928 the Bath Road was diverted to make a bypass on the north side of the village, now part of the A4.

One of the most famous Twyford stories concerns Edward Polehampton, a poor boy who was befriended by the landlord of The Rose and Crown at Christmas in about 1666. Thanks to the help of his new friend, Edward managed to make his way to London, where he made good and became rich. He never forgot his stay in Twyford, and left money in his will to help other poor boys of the village. The Wee Waif Inn is named after him and you will find the Polehampton name in other places around Twyford, including Polehampton Close where the car park is situated.

★ DISTANCE: About 4 miles.

★ REFRESHMENTS: The Duke of Wellington and the Land's End pubs are on or near the route of the walk.

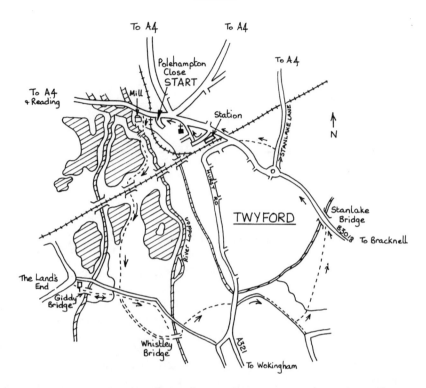

★ HOW TO GET THERE: The walk starts in the car park in Polehampton Close off the High Street in Twyford on the A3032, just prior to the traffic lights if you are coming from the A4 (Wee Waif public house). There are plenty of parking spaces and there are toilets here as well.

★ THE WALK: Turn left out of the car park into the High Street and cross the bridge over the railway line which carries the local Twyford to Henley train. After passing some old terraced houses, turn immediately left through a yard adjacent to the mill. (Many mills have occupied this site, the present one was built in 1979.) A red arrow on the wall points to the footpath.

Next cross a little footbridge, then further on cross a sluice gate. Follow the footpath until you reach a seven-arch bridge, cross the stile and continue to the end of the path then turn right on to the road.

36

If you want to visit the Land's End public house, turn right and in a few steps, just under a sign 'Caution Farm Vehicles', turn left into a small path. Cross the footbridge, go over the stile, then cross the field diagonally to cross a further bridge – 'Giddy Bridge' – to pass along the back of the Land's End. After your stop, retrace your steps back to where you came out on the road.

Carry on up the road for a few steps, to enter a raised path running alongside the road, and follow this to the end. Cross over a stile and turn right. A few yards further on you cross Whistley Bridge and you will soon see a footpath sign across some gravel workings on your left. Follow the signs until you come out on another road. Cross this main road carefully and go over the stile. Keep to the left-hand side of the field and just follow this until you come to yet another stile. There are usually horses in this field, but they are very friendly! Cross the stile and turn right after going over a little bridge.

A few yards down this track turn left to cross the field. Go over a steel bridge, turn left and keep to the path. This is a very good place for blackberries so, if you come at the right time, bring plenty of bags. Carry on along the path and cross a sleeper bridge. Turn right over a stile to keep along the edge of two fields (noting the huge oak in the second field) to reach the road.

Here turn left, to go over Stanlake Bridge and carry on up the road for a while until you reach Stanlake Road. Turn right and shortly go through a gate into the recreation ground. This is called Stanlake Meadow and was acquired from Stanlake Park Estate in 1979 by Twyford Parish Council, as a public open space. Cross to the far right-hand corner and come out on to the road, then cross the road and go over the railway bridge. Turn immediately left down a small footpath to reach the station, go along the platform and come out at a gate at the end into Station Road.

Station Road was built after the arrival of the railway in 1838, and used to be a footpath. It was years before any houses or shops were built here, but in 1898 it became a substantial shopping area, with at least 14 shops. Off Station Road is Gas Lane, named after the Twyford Gas Works which stood here until they were demolished in 1933.

37

Turn left and carry on down the road, past the Old Church of St Mary, built in 1847. The tower was not added until 1910 and a peal of bells was hung in 1913; the tenor bell was named 'George' to commemorate the Coronation of George V.

When you reach the traffic lights, turn left and you will soon be back at your car.

10
THREE MILE CROSS
AND SHINFIELD

---------------★---------------

★ INTRODUCTION: From Three Mile Cross this pleasant walk across open fields and farmland makes its way to the attractive village of Shinfield, with its 15th century cottages beside the church and 16th century manor house.

Three Mile Cross and Shinfield will be familiar territory to anyone who has read Mary Mitford's 'Our Village', sketches of village life which were first collected together in 1824. The house where she lived in Three Mile Cross is marked by a plaque and is passed at the beginning of the walk. Her father was a spendthrift and a gambler and it was left to Mary to support her family by her writing, which gained great popularity in her lifetime and continues to find devotees. Her parents were buried at Shinfield church, where the brass plaque commemorating them lay forgotten for many years beneath the tiles near the font and was only rediscovered in 1936. Mary Mitford herself was buried at Swallowfield, where she lived for the last few years of her life, dying in 1855.

★ DISTANCE: Just under 4 miles.

★ REFRESHMENTS: There are two public houses in Shinfield, The Royal Oak and The Bell and Bottle. both serve lunches and evening meals. At the top of Brookers Hill on the Shinfield Road is The Black Boy, and there is also The Swan in Three Mile Cross.

★ HOW TO GET THERE: The walk starts south of the M4 at Junction 11, on the A33 Old Basingstoke Road at Three Mile

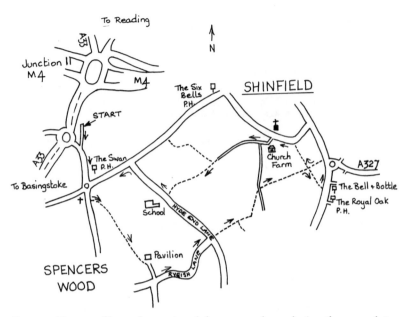

Cross. Turn off at the roundabout and park in the road to your left.

★ THE WALK: Set off away from the A33 towards Spencers Wood, passing on your left the house where Mary Mitford lived and wrote. There is a plaque on the wall, and another on the left-hand side of the door of The Swan, next door. At the mini-roundabout cross straight over. On the right is a pretty cottage – Highway Cottage – which was once a public house called The George and Dragon.

Opposite the telephone box is a footpath on your left. Climb over the stile and keep to the right of the field until you reach another stile, just right of the gate. Walk uphill keeping to the left of the field. About 100 yards up is a gate and from here is a good view of Reading and Berkshire Council Offices, built in 1980.

At the top of the field, go over the stile and skirt Ryeish Green school playing fields. Keeping to the left, still with the playing fields to your left, walk between bushes and undergrowth. Go over the stile and bear left with the sports pavilion on your left – the path leads from the pavilion along the drive, past a pond on your right, to the road. Turn sharp left after passing through the gate.

Now follow this country lane until you reach the T-junction at Ryeish Lane and Hyde End Lane. Cross straight over and follow the fenced footpath, ignoring the path to the right. On reaching the crosspaths (a concrete drive), cross over following the footpath. Go over the stile and keep left of the field until you reach a crosspath to Shinfield. Looking across, there are some new offices called 'Shinfield House' built in 1988. Then head for the car park and the village green with its locally famous oak tree, planted in 1756.

The old school on your right dates from 1707. It was added to in 1847, the clock erected in 1858 and the whole extended in 1889. It is now the village primary school. On the opposite side of the road are the two public houses, The Royal Oak and The Bell and Bottle.

With Shinfield House to your left, walk towards the roundabout – a newsagent's shop is on your right. Bear left at the roundabout and walk along the main road for roughly 50 yards, then turn left on to a footpath just past the police station. Go over the stile, cross (you have been here before), turn right over another stile and turn left at Stantons. On your right is the Old Manor House.

The cottages alongside St Mary's churchyard were built in 1488 and originally formed The Six Bells public house, named after the six bells in the church tower. The pub is now located on Church Lane at the foot of Brookers Hill and is named The Hungry Horse. St Mary's church has been a place of worship since 1069, when the present church was founded by William Fitz Osborne, who was given the manor by William the Conqueror. The brick and flint church has been added to and altered since Norman times and contains many different styles of architecture. During the Civil War a local skirmish between Parliamentarian troops and Royalists resulted in the Royalists taking cover in the church. Cannon fire reduced the tower to rubble, but luckily work was soon begun to restore it and three of its six bells were installed to mark the Restoration of Charles II.

Continuing the walk, turn left along a footpath opposite the church and after approximately 50 yards, at the Farm Office, turn right. Follow the footpath to the fork, keep to the left-hand path and you will emerge opposite Ryeish Green comprehensive school. At this point, turn right and continue until you reach a T-junction, then turn left. Carry on along this road until you get to the mini-roundabout at Three Mile Cross, turn to the right and you will soon be back at your car.

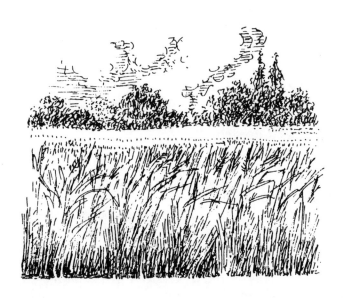

11

THE BLACKWATER
VALLEY
★

★ INTRODUCTION: This is an enjoyable walk from
Swallowfield along the meandering Blackwater where spring
flowers bloom early in sheltered hollows and hedgerows are
alive with birds, with views across meadows and cornfields.
The return route past Sandpits Farm leads to a gentle uphill
walk across fields to be rewarded with a view across the
valley below Farley Hill.

The name Swallowfield is derived from Old German mean-
ing 'rushing water', and the river Blackwater is only one of
three rivers that flow through the valley; the walk passes the
confluence of the Blackwater with the Whitewater. This area
was once part of Windsor Great Forest and is still pleasantly
wooded. The Roman road from Silchester to London runs
through the parish and, known today as the Devil's Highway,
it crosses the river Blackwater at Thatcher's Ford.

★ DISTANCE: The walk is 3¾ miles. If, however, you are
walking in wet weather, the track below Wyvols Copse can
become deeply muddy and you may wish to use country
lanes as an alternative, shortening or lengthening the walk as
you choose – details are given in the route of the walk.

★ REFRESHMENTS: The George and Dragon, Swallowfield, The
Crown, The Street, Swallowfield, and the Fox and Hounds,
Farley Hill.

★ HOW TO GET THERE: Swallowfield lies about 2½ miles

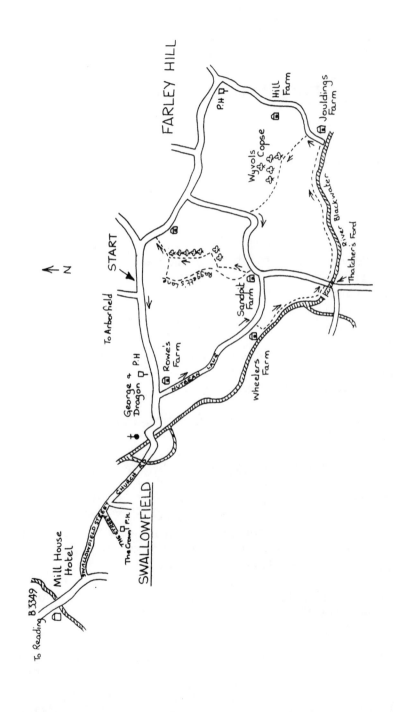

south of Junction 11 on the M4 motorway, signposted A33. At the next roundabout, however, ignore the dual carriageway ahead and turn left onto the old road through the villages of Three Mile Cross and Spencers Wood (B3349). Beyond Spencers Wood the twisting road passes The Mill House Hotel, on your right. Take the next left-hand turn into Swallowfield Street, signposted to Swallowfield. Continue on past the Parish Hall and The Red Lodge, on your left, where the road becomes Church Road. The grounds of Swallowfield Park are on the left and there are two hump-backed bridges, the second on a sharp bend by the parish church of All Saints. After another sharp bend the straighter road passes The George and Dragon on your left, then a road to Arborfield, also on the left. Just beyond the junction there is a gravel verge with parking space for several cars (GR 742648).

★ THE WALK: Take the road back in the direction you have just come and turn left along Nutbean Lane. After passing Wheeler's Farm, on your right, turn right off the road at a footpath sign waymarked with a yellow arrow. Cross the footbridge and stile onto a grassy path enclosed by trees and hedges. Follow the path to a stile into a field and turn left to walk alongside the Blackwater river. Beyond the point where the Whitewater joins the Blackwater there is a footbridge over the river. Ignore this and take the left-hand fork in the path towards a stile beside a metal gate in the corner of the field. Go over the stile and cross the road. (The walk can be considerably shortened by taking the lane north to Sandpits Farm from Thatcher's Ford.)

Cross the rising ground beyond to another stile waymarked with a yellow arrow in continuation of the recreational route. Follow the path, keeping the hedge on your right, and follow on through the fields, alongside the hedgerow with the river beyond. Bear slightly right at the corner of each field to pass between the hedges to the small footbridges crossing ditches and over stiles. Emerging into a field with more open views across the river on your right, the red brick Jouldings Farm can be seen at the far corner. Continue along the river bank, going to the left at the end of the field to a stile in the hedge onto Jouldings Lane. Turn left along

45

the road, leaving behind Jouldings Farm and the continuation of the Blackwater Valley recreational route. (If you wish to look at Jouldings Ford this is a five minute return journey from this point.)

After 100 yards up the lane take a track to the left beside a bank with a metal gate and a view of Hill Farm on the rising ground beyond. This track past Wyvols Copse is much used by horse riders and gets deeply muddy in wet weather. To avoid this, the longer option rises steeply up Jouldings Lane, used by the army for training exercises. You may be glad you are not required to run up with full pack and grateful to see The Fox and Hounds public house at the top. To return to Sandpits Farm, continue left, through the village, then left again into Sandpit Lane. A further option is to keep to the road ahead and down the hill back to the start (see sketch map).

If continuing the walk as shown, follow the track through until it rises to join the narrow Sandpit Lane. Turn left here and, ignoring tracks on the left and footpath signs on the right, continue along the winding lane until you reach a grassy track on the right, with the garden hedge of Sandpits Farm alongside to the left of the track. Go ahead to a stile beside a wooden gate. There is an ancient, enclosed green lane to the left of the gate.

The waymarked footpath beyond the wooden gate, over the stile, gives more open views than will be afforded by the old lane. Walk across the meadow to a gap in the trees at the top of the hill. In the corner, beside a large oak tree, you will find an unusual, long double stile. Cross this and turn right and then left along the field edge with a fence and trees on the right. At a raised headland path flanked by five spaced oak trees, turn left downhill to a stile beside a metal gate. At the footpath sign ahead, turn right. This is the other end of the ancient Raggetts Lane. Follow through between hedges to join the road. Turn left along the road, back to the start.

12
FINCHAMPSTEAD

————————————★————————————

★ INTRODUCTION: This exhilarating walk through undulating countryside offering splendid views, ancient woodland which was once part of Windsor Great Forest, and water meadows near the river Blackwater, is based upon the attractive village of Finchampstead.

Finchampstead has a long and fascinating history. The Roman road from Silchester to Staines, now known as the Devil's Highway, runs through the parish and in the garden at Banisters, a 15th/16th century timber-framed house, is a Roman pyramidal milestone found on the old road. The ancient hill upon which the original church of St James was built was formerly a signal station of the Roman legions.

The oldest memorial in the church is to Henry Hinde, Purveyor at Court, who survived the religious changes of the Tudor period and served Henry VIII, Edward VI, Mary and Elizabeth I. Another link with the Tudor period is on Fair Green, where a sign made from an old yew tree relates that on 6th November 1501, Henry VII was told that the young Spanish princess Catherine of Aragon was at Dogmersfield. Henry and his sons, Prince Arthur and Prince Henry, rode to meet her at The Ridges, and to escort her to London.

★ DISTANCE: About 3½ miles. OS Map Landranger Sheet 175.

★ REFRESHMENTS: Available at The Greyhound Inn at the junction of the B3016 and the B3348, and the Queen's Oak close to St James's church.

★ HOW TO GET THERE: From Wokingham take the A321 sign-posted to Sandhurst, then the B3016 to Finchampstead. Keep

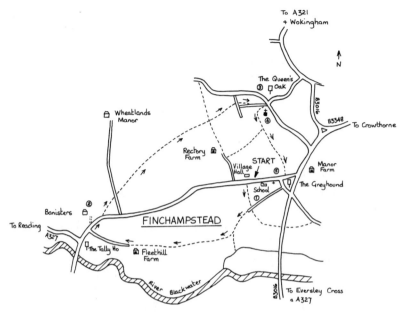

right onto the B3348 into 'The Village'. The walk commences from the verge in front of the recreational area of the Finchampstead Memorial Park, where there is limited parking.

★ THE WALK: With your back to the park, cross the road and walk to the right. Immediately after the garage, turn left on to a footpath between fences on the left and a hedge on the right.

At the end of the path, our walk turns to the right, but about 20 yards to the left is the sign on Fair Green which commemorates Henry VII's presence here.

Retrace your steps to the junction and continue along the path with ancient woodland on the right – sycamore, hazel, cherry, oak and holly. The ditch on the left has deposits of red iron oxide and is a link with the past when iron ore was smelted in the area. Take the next footpath signed to the right over the stile into a field.

Continue along the edge of the field, with the wood on the right. At the field boundary is a stile; continue over it in the same direction along a track which leads through farm buildings and eventually to the main road. Turn right, take care crossing the road and walk along the grass verge, passing the entrance to Banisters and South Lodge. At the end of the wattle fence on the left, pass through a wooden gate and walk half right across the field to the gate, keeping the fence on your left. To the left over the field is Banisters.

Cross over the drive to Wheatlands Manor, over a stile and walk along a fenced path. This area was part of the Windsor Great Forest and as you continue there are splendid views over the fields towards Finchampstead church, partially obscured by hedges.

At the junction of the paths, continue ahead with the hedge on the left. After the stile cross the lane to a track, keeping to the left of the pine tree. Beyond White Horse House and the entrance to the Manor House, is a listed 17th century wall. Cross the green to the church entrance, passing the red oak which was planted to commemorate the Silver Jubilee of George V.

If sustenance is required, fork left to the Queen's Oak Inn. This public house was previously called The White Horse. It is a listed building of about the late 18th century, but it is probable that there has been a hostelry on the site since Roman times.

The steep banking to the south and east of the church is part of an old earthwork, which the Romans made use of. It is here, in the 7th century, that the Saxon settlers received the Christian faith from Bishop Birinus. They built a wooden church which has long since vanished but left an interesting stone font with cable carving. The round apse and small arch dividing the nave from the chancel are Norman. The north aisle was added in two periods as shown by the different windows and roof timbers. The west end of this aisle is believed to have been a chantry chapel for the Banister family. Further additions to the church were made in 1590. The brick tower, with corner pinnacles, was erected in 1720 and has six bells.

Pass through the wooden gate into the churchyard and bear right, keeping the church on the left. On approaching a tree, take the path to the right, down some brick steps and leave the churchyard through the kissing gate.

Continue along this path, ignoring the footpath sign to the right. From the top of the hill you can see the playing fields of the Memorial Park. At the end of the footpath turn right into 'The Village'. It is advisable to cross over the road and walk on the pavement. To the left is the other hostelry, The Greyhound. There has been a pub here since the 17th century, but the present building only dates back to the end of the 19th century.

Continue along the street; opposite Longwater Lane is The Forge and The Thatched Cottage. The latter, a 17th century building, has an interesting history, having been home to a poltergeist a few years ago, until it was eventually exorcised and peace restored. Just past the Baptist church on the left is The Verge, another listed building, and in a few yards you are back at the starting point.

13
MORTIMER

───────────────★───────────────

★ INTRODUCTION: This pleasant walk from the ancient village of Mortimer takes you over its historic common, known as the Fairground, and across open fields and woodland to the north of the village. At one point the view opens out to include five counties – on a clear day!

Mortimer is a village of just over 3,000 population, with thriving churches, schools and shops. In earlier days it was known for its wood-working industries and evidence of old-time coppicing may still be seen in the woods. The Common, properly called the Fairground, was once used for the regular horse fairs. These, and the Welsh cattle fairs, were held in May and November each year, bringing beasts and drovers from far and wide. The Fairground is still used by travelling fairs and circuses, as well as by the village for charity fairs.

St John's church, at the start of the walk, is the younger of Mortimer's two parish churches – the other, St Mary's, dates originally from Saxon times. St John's was built in 1881 to save the villagers who lived around the common the long walk down the hill to church every week.

★ DISTANCE: About 3½ miles.

★ REFRESHMENTS: Mortimer is well endowed with public houses which offer meals and refreshments throughout the day.

★ HOW TO GET THERE: From the A4 Bath Road take the turning through Burghfield. From Junction 11 of the M4 take the A33 towards Basingstoke and the third exit at the next roundabout. The walk starts at St John's church in the centre of the village where there is car parking.

★ THE WALK: From the car park in front of St John's church, go over the road to the Common and take a diagonal path to the kissing-gate at the far right-hand corner, passing between the children's playground and the tennis courts and cricket field. Cross the road on the right and enter the woods, keeping to the left on the path. This brings you to an open field where you take the left of the two paths to cross the middle of the field. Continue alongside a fence in the second field until you emerge onto a small country road opposite Manns Farm. The public footpath originally went through the yard of the farm, but due to vandalism in the past, this path may only be used after obtaining permission to do so at the farm. To find the public footpath, turn right as you come onto the road and the path is well signposted about 100 yards on the left.

Go through the small wood to come out onto an open field, the three sides of which you walk, starting by going to the right and then along the bottom hedge. The third side is over the stile and left uphill on the further side of the hedge. At the top of the hill you join the track you would have taken

MORTIMER

52

from Manns Farmyard, and you should pause here to enjoy the view. On a clear day, you can see five counties. On the horizon to the left is a fine row of Wellingtonia pines and the nearer cream building, of which one sees mainly the much extended back and side area, is Wokefield Park. It is now a conference centre but was once St Benedict's School and a borstal.

Turn right along the track and, in a few yards, sharp left over a stile to go downhill, passing beside a blasted tree, to a gate and a small pond. Leaving the pond on the left, climb the stile and bear right along the edge of the field to go over a small brook by a stile and a bridge. The footpath now goes straight uphill across the middle of the field (sometimes the course of the path is marked only by the trace of previous walkers through the thick grass). On reaching the road turn left for about ¼ mile. The road is tree-lined until at a right-angled bend it opens out with a field on the left. Just after passing three large houses, also on the left, with immaculate lawns edging the road, another road joins and you take the track on the left past Pound Green Cottages and go on through the woods. The path continues on across a road, but where later it takes a broad sweep to the right, go sharp left before Starvale House. The path is signposted and is through a gate and between fences to take you back into woods. Continue until you reach a junction of paths, where you turn left and eventually come out onto a road.

The direct way back to St John's church is to continue straight ahead on the road, at the end of which you will see, slightly to the left, the Common and St John's Church at the far side. Alternatively, turn right and cross the road to a path to the right of Bridges Farm. This path will lead you to an area of pine trees through which you bear right to arrive at Windmill Road. By going to the right and around the bend you will have the choice of The Carpenters Arms or The Victoria Arms if you are in need of refreshment, and will be close to the starting point.

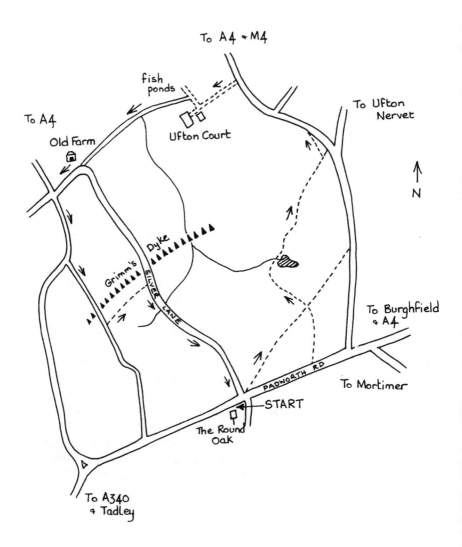

14

A WOODLAND WALK AROUND UFTON

─────────────★─────────────

★ INTRODUCTION: Although less than 10 miles from Basingstoke or Reading, this walk provides woodland paths, lakeside views and vistas of open countryside. The highlight, however, is that it passes through the grounds of Ufton Court and allows a close look at the Elizabethan house.

The present Ufton Court was completed in 1576 by the Perkins family. They were a steadfast Roman Catholic family and, during the religious persecution in Elizabeth I's reign, the Court became a 'safe house' for Catholic priests. Six hiding places and an escape tunnel were made, of which five priest holes and part of the tunnel still remain today. Later the house was badly neglected but it was restored in 1880. Today it is used by the Local Education Authority for residential courses but the public may visit it on open days.

The Oval Pond is the home of ducks and moorhens but perhaps the most fascinating forms of wildlife are the blue damselflies which dart around the lakeside in the summer.

Silver Lane was the scene of an 18th century murder when an old man was beaten to death. Two men were sentenced in Reading and their bodies hung in chains not far from the scene of the crime for many years.

★ DISTANCE: The walk is only 4 miles but there are many points of interest which make this walk suitable for a half-day excursion.

★ REFRESHMENTS: The Round Oak public house provides light lunches which may be taken in the bar or the garden.

★ HOW TO GET THERE: The walk starts and ends in the car park of The Round Oak, Padworth Common which is on the road from Burghfield Common to Tadley.

★ THE WALK: From The Round Oak turn right, then cross the road and follow it for a few yards to the crossroads. Take the signed footpath which begins at the corner of the main road and the left-hand lane. Follow the wide woodland path until it is crossed by a similar wide path. Turn left and keep going for several hundred yards, following the path round to the right at the next junction. The lake is soon reached.

The path forks immediately beyond the lake. Keep left and eventually a country lane can be seen ahead. Just before reaching the road turn left into a narrow path which immediately dips down to a ditch before ascending the other side to an open woodland path. At the end of the path turn right, crossing the hedge ditch to the country road. Turn left and follow the road until the entrance to Ufton Court is reached. Turn left down the drive (which is also a public footpath), observing the excellent views across the Kennet valley on the left and Ufton Court in front. Just before the house turn right between the lawns for a few yards, then turn left into a dark, woody lane marked 'Footpath'.

A short distance down the lane it is possible to see on the left the remains of a series of medieval fish ponds. The lane gradually descends to a stream before climbing again to a gate marking the entrance to Old Farm. Please remember to close the gate. Cross the farmyard, joining the road at an L-bend. Do not turn left but continue straight ahead.

Follow the lane to the crossroads. Turn left and continue along the road until it makes a sharp right bend. On the left are two paths, take the second which is a narrow woodland path. Ignore an immediate left turn and further on the path runs hard by a high wire fence. Take the next signposted path on the left and follow this until the road is reached. Turn right into Silver Lane and continue to the main road where the walk began. Turn right and The Round Oak is clearly visible.

15
PADWORTH AND THE KENNET AND AVON CANAL

————————————★————————————

★ INTRODUCTION: An easy and fascinating walk along part of the long distance footpath which follows the recently restored Kennet and Avon Canal. Allow plenty of time to enjoy the activity on the canal and to take in the fine views of the Kennet valley on the return journey.

Completed early in the 19th century, the canal is part of a waterway system which links the town of Reading with the city of Bristol. At Lower Padworth there is now a small shop and visitor centre selling books, maps and souvenirs.

Padworth church and nearby Padworth House lie up the hill across the meadows from the river Kennet. It is said that long ago a man working at Padworth House had an affair with the owner's wife, whose husband had him killed and the body thrown into the water. You might even encounter his ghost riding down the hill!

★ DISTANCE: Approximately 4 miles of easy going, but allow time to watch the narrowboats at Padworth Lock and rest on the seat that circles the old yew tree in the churchyard.

★ REFRESHMENTS: The Visitor Centre, on your right as you approach the Aldermaston lift bridge, is open from April until October for light refreshments. The Butt Inn on the A340 is a short walk (200 yards) ahead as you cross the Aldermaston lift bridge.

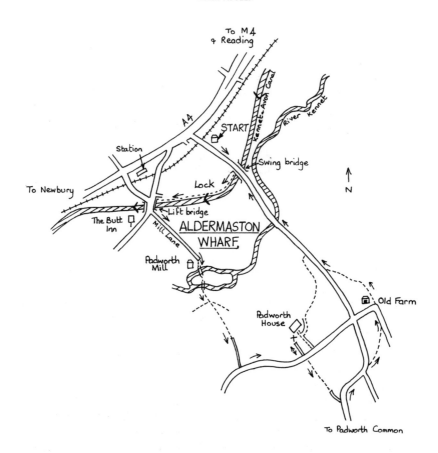

★ HOW TO GET THERE: The walk starts at Padworth village hall (GR 608684). Take the Padworth turn off the A4. The hall is on the left beyond the railway bridge. By public transport: Rail – check the timetable (0345 484950). An infrequent service runs between Reading and Newbury. Not all trains stop at Aldermaston. Start the walk at Aldermaston lift bridge. Take the south exit from the station (over the footbridge if travelling from the direction of Newbury). Turn left out of the car park and then right to the bridge. By bus – take the 102 along A4 from Reading or Newbury, alight at Padworth and follow directions for car. Travellers' timetable – 01635 40743.

★ THE WALK: Leave the hall and turn left along the road. Do not cross the Padworth swing bridge over the canal, but turn right along the towpath. Padworth Lock will soon come into view. It was restored in 1983. Beyond the lock, on the opposite bank, you will see the Malthouses. Grain used to be stored here before being taken up the lane to the mill. In 1936 they were converted into private houses. The poet Richard Aldington lived in the Maltster's Cottage in the 1920s and was visited here by his friends T.S. Eliot and D.H. Lawrence. On your right at Padworth Lower Wharf is the visitors' centre.

Turn left over the Aldermaston lift bridge and fork left immediately down Mill Lane, leaving Bridge House on your left. The cottages on the left were built by Strange's Brewery. Look for the plaque on the wall. The cottages and the Malthouses had their water supplied free by the brewery, which used to be on the south side of the canal.

Turn right along a narrow footpath immediately beyond the entrance to the trout farm. This takes you between the trout farm and Padworth Mill. Follow the path across the bridges. Climb the stile into the meadow and make for the gap in the hedge ahead and cross a second meadow to a stile directly ahead (do not take the path diagonally left which may be better defined). Cross the stile and the bridge and climb gently through the wood. At the road, turn left. Continue along the road until you reach the track leading to Padworth church. The Norman church is well worth a visit. There are fragments of a 13th century wall painting on the south side of the chancel arch. During restoration work in 1982 the coffins of Christopher and Catherine Griffiths were found. They had lived at Padworth House (now a college), built in 1759, close to the church.

Walk back to the road and pass through a kissing gate opposite. Walk up the field, keeping the boundary on your right, pass through into a second field, the boundary will now be on your left. Walk through a gate and onto a drive. On reaching the road, turn left. Continue a short way along the road until it bends sharply left. Walk straight ahead, taking the footpath opposite which heads diagonally across a field. When you come out onto the road, turn left. Cross over at the sharp left-hand bend into the farmyard opposite. There are three footpaths signposted here. Take the path on the left which goes between the farm buildings and becomes a broad track leading downhill between fields. From here there are extensive views across the Kennet valley. You can see Englefield House ahead in the distance and catch a glimpse of the chimneys of Ufton Court to the right. It is rumoured that there is a tunnel from the Court to Padworth.

At the bottom of the hill, cross onto a narrow path. Turn left and follow the path to the road. Turn right along the road and return to the village hall, crossing first the river Kennet and then the canal.

16
WOOLHAMPTON AND MIDGHAM
★

★ INTRODUCTION: In the beautiful Kennet valley, this relaxing walk follows the towpath of the Kennet and Avon Canal, with the chance of spotting heron and kingfisher, before climbing to Midgham House and its ancient trees and parkland.

The Rowbarge Inn, at the start of the walk, is over 400 years old and would have catered for the needs of river traffic after the canalisation of the Kennet between 1715 and 1723. Woolhampton's history has long been bound up with travel and trade, the Kennet valley holding not only the river but also the Kennet and Avon Canal, the old Bath Road (A4) and the railway. There is a great deal of interest to be discovered in the village, including old inns, a commemorative fountain and an ancient mill.

The original Midgham House was demolished in 1967 and all that remains today is the greenery-clad portico which formed part of the front entrance; the coach house and stables have been converted to living accommodation. A new Midgham House has been built in the former gardens overlooking the lakes. Another old manor house passed on the walk is Hall Court, held in the early 14th century by John Hall. For a time it functioned as a vicarage, until 1936 when a new vicarage was built in Midgham.

★ DISTANCE: 3¾ miles, the first part being fairly flat along the canal; the only real hill of note is Church Hill.

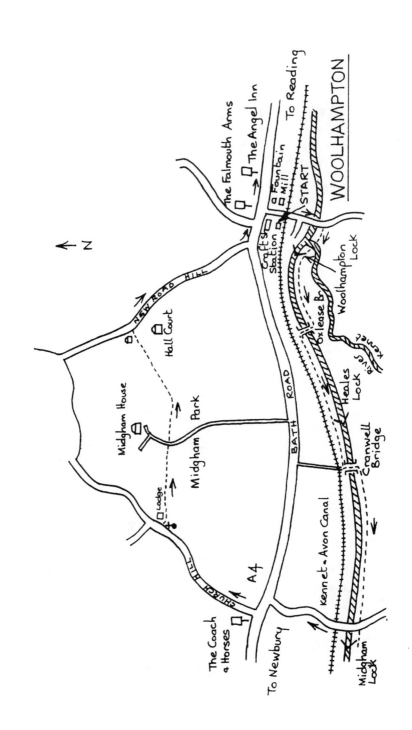

★ REFRESHMENTS: The Rowbarge Inn serves bar meals both at lunchtime until 2 pm and in the evening from 7 pm to 10 pm. The Angel Inn, Woolhampton and The Coach and Horses at Midgham also serve lunches and bar meals during opening hours.

★ HOW TO GET THERE: Take the A4 to Woolhampton and turn down the road opposite the Angel Inn. You can either park in the station car park or at The Rowbarge car park by the canal if 'out of opening hours' (if you decide to do the latter, join the walk at the beginning of the second paragraph below).

★ THE WALK: From the car park entrance to Midgham Station, proceed across the level crossing. The station was once 'Woolhampton Station', but had to be renamed in 1873 to prevent confusion with Wolverhampton. Continue on until you have crossed the swingbridge over the river Kennet, then turn right on to the towpath.

This section of the path was known at the beginning of the century as the Rope Walk, and was where rope was made. Cross the footbridge, under which the Kennet flows from the left, and then continue on the towpath past the rebuilt Woolhampton Lock into the parish of Midgham. The canal bank and water margins support a rich plant life, and listen out for the first calling of the cuckoo from the willow trees on the left.

Walk on along the towpath until you reach Oxlease Bridge. To the left there used to be a cowslip meadow, now gravel extraction has made a lake which is destined to be a nature reserve. Local conservationists replanted many of the cowslips where they would not be disturbed. Cross over the bridge, for the towpath now crosses to the north bank. Look out for herons amongst the reeds, yellow iris and purple loosestrife, or the blue flash of the kingfisher.

Heale's Lock lies ahead, recently rebuilt and replacing a turf-sided lock which had fallen into disrepair. The towpath crosses back to the south bank at the next swingbridge, named Cranwell Bridge (pronounced locally 'Crannel'). Having crossed the bridge a lush green meadow lies to the

63

left, destined to become another lake following gravel extraction. Eventually trees on the northern bank will give way to open meadows and Midgham church can be seen on the top of the hill overlooking the Kennet valley, a landmark for travellers by road, rail and water since 1869.

Pass beneath the Midgham-Brimpton road bridge to Midgham Lock. Leave the towpath here by walking up the incline, then having passed through the gate turn left and proceed along the road to the junction with the A4 Bath Road.

Cross the A4 to The Coach and Horses public house. This is approximately halfway along the route of the walk. Proceed up the road to the right of the pub (Church Hill) until you reach a wooden seat on the right by the church gate.

Leave the road through the gate by West Lodge (signposted), taking the footpath up the Lodge drive between the house and the church, through Midgham Park. On entering the park, please remember to close all gates after you and keep your dog on a lead as livestock often graze here. Follow the ancient track through trees and a hollow. The history of the manor dates from the first half of the 13th century, when it was held by Giles Erley and it remained in the hands of his family for over 450 years. In 1738 it was bought by Stephen Poyntz, a diplomat and later tutor to George II's son William, Duke of Cumberland, for whom a suite of rooms were added. Stephen's daughter, Georgiana, married John Spencer, later 1st Earl Spencer of Althorpe, ancestor of Princess Diana.

Go through the gate and continue straight along, keeping the hedge/fence to the left and passing through other gates until you reach the gravel drive leading to Midgham House. Cross the drive to enter the meadow opposite, and walk across this towards a slight incline and a gated fence. The site of the old chapel, replaced by St Matthew's church, surrounded by its overgrown graveyard lies to the right of the brick ha-ha, but is now hidden from view.

In the next meadow the path goes slightly left between two small hillocks, followed by further gates/stiles until you reach the road by East Lodge. Note the fine hornbeam tree on the other side of the road.

Turn right and proceed down the road. Having passed a small copse of deciduous and pine trees on the right, another former manor house can be seen standing back from the road, Hall Court. This is a relatively quiet country road, between meadow and woodland, but nearer Woolhampton development has taken place on either side. At the junction with the A4, turn left and walk along the pavement crossing the bottom of Woolhampton Hill to The Falmouth Arms. Known as the 'Upper Angel' in the early 19th century, it became The Falmouth Arms when the 4th Viscount Falmouth was lord of the manor of Woolhampton.

Pass the village shop to the forecourt of the Angel Inn. The present building was erected in 1931 when the old coaching inn, along with a harness shop, butcher's shop and slaughter-house, a malt house and other long established buildings were demolished for road widening. Cross the A4 to the timber framed Tudor cottage or craft shop and turn into Station Road.

The Fountain on the opposite corner was erected in 1897 to commemorate Queen Victoria's Jubilee and provide the village with a water supply from an artesian well, other than that from the river. The red brick house with its tower was once the home of the miller whose grist mill can also be seen on the other side of the road, complete with its water wheel. There was certainly a mill here in the 14th century and it is possible that one may have been on this site since before the Domesday Book.

Another few yards will bring you back to the starting point of the walk at the station car park.

17
CHAPEL ROW
AND
BUCKLEBURY COMMON
━━━━━━━━━━━★━━━━━━━━━━━

★ INTRODUCTION: This fascinating walk combines a variety
of scenery and wildlife habitats with ancient commonland
and historic sites, including a medieval dovecote and 13th
century fishponds. You may be lucky enough to see the
muntjac and roedeer that roam this area, or even signs of
badgers and foxes, while the resident bird species are
augmented in summer by many migrants, most notably
nightingales and nightjars.

Bucklebury common escaped enclosure in the 19th century and villagers continued to graze their animals there into
comparatively recent times. During the Civil War, before the
second battle of Newbury in 1644, some 20,000 Parliamentarian troops were camped on the common.

Bucklebury is well known for its oak trees, particularly
those in the famous avenue, the first of which were planted
to commemorate a visit by Elizabeth I. More plantings were
made to mark national occasions such as the victory at
Waterloo and royal celebrations.

★ DISTANCE: About 4 miles. Stout shoes are needed, summer
and winter, as areas of heavy clay can be wet, and some of
the tracks are used as bridlepaths.

★ REFRESHMENTS: There are no refreshments available on the
walk itself, but at Chapel Row, your starting and finishing

point, the Bladebone Inn will revive you at the end of your trek. Opening times are 10.30 am to 2.30 pm, and 5.30 pm to 11 pm. They would like notice if a large number of walkers intend calling in.

★ HOW TO GET THERE: The simplest way is from the A4 between Reading and Newbury. Coming from Newbury, drive through Thatcham and turn left to Bucklebury when you see it signposted. This will take you up the hill into Upper Bucklebury. Continue along this road, across the common, until you reach the next settlement, which is Chapel Row, your starting point. Coming from Reading direction, you will drive through a stretch of dual carriageway at Beenham. A mile further on turn right (the turning is on a left bend, so be prepared) and after nearly 2 miles turn right again to Chapel Row. There is no actual car park, but a layby can accommodate several cars.

★ THE WALK: From Chapel Row head north-west, following the Stanford Dingley road or the open space beside it. Very shortly you will come to a pond in a clump of trees. Keep the pond, the haunt of many dragonflies and damselflies, on the right and bear left at the fork, following a waymarked byway. Join a drive and pass some houses on the right before reaching a junction. Turn right and then right again after a few yards, by a byway sign, following the track beside houses. On reaching the drive to a house on the right, join a path dropping down into a wooded gully in front of you. Many woodland birds can be seen here, and a quiet advance should be well rewarded. On reaching the road, turn left. Bird watchers will still find it interesting, with woods on their left and open farmland on the right, and many flowers abound in the hedges.

A short walk will bring you to the pound, on the left of the road, where straying cattle used to be penned in the days when the commoners still grazed cattle on the common. Another ½ mile or so will bring you to the edge of Bucklebury village. On your left you will see the old Victorian school house, now converted to a private dwelling. On the right are some very old farm buildings, partly brought up to

67

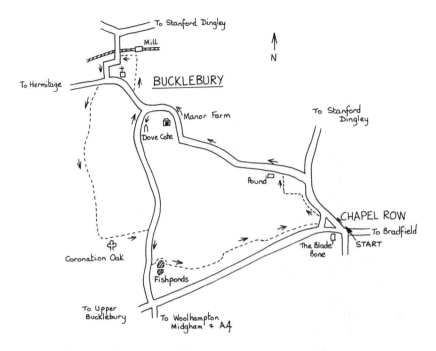

date, but with some obvious joinery proclaiming their origins, probably in the late 16th or early 17th century.

Rounding the corner you will see Manor Farm on your left, and behind it the old manor house, which has been in the same family for more than 450 years. It is interesting to turn left for a few yards here, to see the medieval dovecote which can accommodate 2,000 birds, and would have provided the family with meat.

Returning to the original road, proceed towards the church, but after the road bends right, pass through some galvanised gates on the right and walk in a northerly direction beside the grounds of the old vicarage. This, too, is now in private hands, as modern vicarages are much more modest! There is a short length of ha-ha on the left of the path. Ahead is the old Mill Barn. The waterwheel, which has been restored in recent years, provided power for the village foundry for 300 years from the 17th century. Alas, the river Pang, upon which the mill stands, is one of Britain's distressed rivers, and is a mere shadow of its former self.

Turning left at the mill you soon rejoin a road, which you follow to the left through houses, some of which are the old forge buildings converted, and some new ones built in a sympathetic style. You then come to a T-junction, and although the route takes you to the right, the church on the left is worth a visit.

Back on the road, travel west for a short distance, turning left into a field path immediately past the last house on the left. This soon diverts into a gully slightly to the left, but continuing southwards up the hill. Coming out of the gully it is worth pausing to admire the views of the Pang valley on either side of the ridge on which you stand.

Further up the hill you come to a stretch of what was once thick woodland, but which was devastated in the storms of 1987 and 1990. This has been colonised by such weeds as ragwort and rosebay willowherb, and is now the haunt of many butterflies and moths.

For the last ½ mile you have been walking along the perimeter of a deer farm, with only a narrow stretch of woodland concealing it. Merge with a track at the top of the hill and continue heading south. Pass a cottage on the right and keep going to the next signposted bridleway on the left. Follow it to a rights of way sign, beyond which is a huge oak tree known as the Coronation Oak. A congregation of 1,000 met here for a service on the day of Edward VII's coronation, afterwards gathering for refreshments at nearby Vanner's Barn, which was unfortunately burnt down during the winter of 1985/86.

Keep the Coronation Oak on the right, passing alongside the deer farm, where red deer can be seen grazing in the fields, and after ¼ mile you reach the road. Turn right, and shortly left opposite the one house on this stretch of road. The path takes you to the fishponds, which date from the 13th century, when they were made by the monks of Reading Abbey, to provide fish for the manor house, which the Abbot established.

Continue past the fish ponds, turning right at the next bridleway sign to join a drive by the entrance to a house. Turn left at the next byway sign and follow the power lines. Cross several tracks and keep going in an easterly direction, in line with the power cables. Eventually the Bladebone Inn comes into view. Its sign is reputed to contain the bladebone of a mammoth which was dug up in the Kennet valley nearby. You will be looking forward to refreshments, but pause to look along the road to the east at the famous avenue of oaks.

18
COLD ASH

————————★————————

★ INTRODUCTION: This walk provides spectacular views across the Kennet valley and towards the Pang valley from the area around Cold Ash. Look out for the Wildlife Allotment area on your return route, which attracts a wide range of wildlife and is managed by volunteers.

Cold Ash is a straggling village on a coniferous sandy ridge north-east of Newbury, where the land rises to about 500 ft above sea level. At the turn of the century it was still a typical rural village, with most of the inhabitants employed locally; the population has gradually increased and some larger houses have been demolished and replaced by small estates.

There is a fine Victorian church of local red brick, and Downe House, a girls public school, is nearby. Acland Hall, where the walk begins, was built on land donated by Sir Richard Acland, whose family had lived in the village for many years.

★ DISTANCE: 4 miles.

★ REFRESHMENTS: The Castle provides excellent refreshments.

★ HOW TO GET THERE: Turn north from the A4 at Thatcham; there are roads at either end of the village which join to lead to Cold Ash. Alternatively turn east, and shortly over a railway line, off the B4009, south of Hermitage. Start from Acland Hall, by the recreation ground; you may park here.

★ THE WALK: From the hall, turn left along Hermitage Road and proceed to the crossroads. Turn left into Fishers Lane.

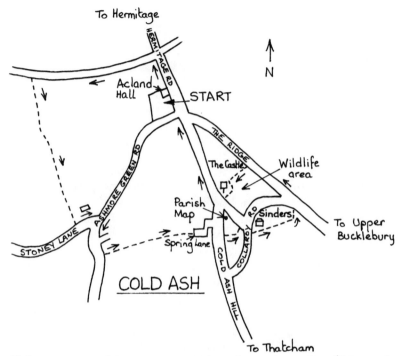

Take care on this narrow road and continue for 650 yards, passing a pumping station on the left. Turn left onto a track at the footpath sign; there is also a 'Private Road' sign on a tree. Pass two dwellings on the right and a stable/outbuildings on the left. Cross the meadow to a gate, and stile in the far corner. From the stile proceed straight ahead, with a fence on your right, until you reach a footpath sign near farm buildings.

Cross the corner of the field to a stile by oak trees on your left. Cross over a bridge and stile; there is a footpath sign on the far side of the stile. Turn right and continue alongside a hedge, with a ditch on the left. Cross the concrete track to a stile and follow the path. On reaching Stoney Lane, turn left and proceed past Ashmore Green Garage to the Y-junction. Turn right into Ashmore Green Road past a road on the left (Ash Terrace). Look for a footpath on the left, and follow this to Spring Lane. Cross Cold Ash Hill to the footpath next to Larch House.

This path emerges into Gladstone Lane, close to the junction with Collaroy Road. Cross the road to a bridleway starting next to 'Sinders'. Continue to the junction with a farm track, then turn left. Follow the track to The Ridge. Turn left, continue along The Ridge, and take the second footpath on the left, next to an electricity transformer.

At the bottom of a slope look for a stile on your left; this is an entrance to the Wildlife Allotment Garden. The garden offers a diversity of habitats, which attract a wide range of wildlife. The area is carefully managed by a group of volunteers.

From the wildlife area rejoin the footpath, continue downhill and you are at The Castle public house. (Note the Parish Map opposite.) Turn right up Cold Ash Hill to return to the recreation ground.

19
CURRIDGE

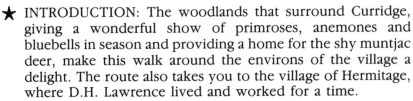

★ INTRODUCTION: The woodlands that surround Curridge, giving a wonderful show of primroses, anemones and bluebells in season and providing a home for the shy muntjac deer, make this walk around the environs of the village a delight. The route also takes you to the village of Hermitage, where D.H. Lawrence lived and worked for a time.

Curridge has had its moments of fame in the past – King John is said to have stopped here when out hunting and, a few centuries later, Oliver Cromwell stayed at Lanolee Farm. Other parts of the village's history, less exciting but probably of more importance to those who lived here, can be traced through local names – Kiln Terrace, for instance, where brickmaking was carried out until the Second World War, and Chapel Lane, where a small chapel, now a dwelling house, once existed.

★ DISTANCE: About 4 miles of country lanes and woodland paths.

★ REFRESHMENTS: The Bunk Inn in Curridge, the Tea Rooms at Hillier's Garden Centre, or The White Horse in Hermitage all offer varied and excellent fare.

★ HOW TO GET THERE: From the Robin Hood roundabout in Newbury, take the B4009 to Hermitage and Streatley. About 4 miles north of Newbury look for the Lamb Inn on the right, and Chieveley Garage on the left. Continue over a slight rise, and pass the Red Shute Hill turning on the right, with the one to Sandy Close on the left. Take the next turning on the left, within 60 yards, to 'Curridge Village and Winterbourne'.

This is the Curridge Road. Continue along here, a tree-lined road, for about ½ mile until you come to a crossroads. Crab Tree lane is on your right, an unsurfaced road where you can park in safety.

★ THE WALK: Walk back to the crossroads, where the signs show Curridge village to the right, and Winterbourne straight ahead. Turn left and walk back along the tree-lined road, passing bungalows, houses and Plantation Close on the left. Two hundred yards past the last bungalow on the left, opposite the post box on a tree, the way leads through a small plantation, rising gently along a hedge-lined path, going almost parallel with the road you have just walked along. At the crest of the hill this passes between a house and chalet bungalow, with a menagerie of ducks, chickens, goats, small pigs, etc and continues down to a tarmac road.

Here turn left and continue along a track, immediately past the gate pillars of the house you passed at the top of the rise. (This track can be very muddy in wet weather; if so it may be better to miss out this triangle of the walk and continue along the road past the WI Hall on the right, and join the other path again at School Lane.)

If you venture along the muddy path, continue up here until you meet a right turn. Take it and continue, passing the bungalows of Curridge Green and riding school on your left, and the Old Parsonage on the right. H.M. Bateman, the cartoonist, once lived here. As you meet the road, turn right and then immediately left to Curridge school at the footpath sign.

This track passes the school, which has an interesting history. Much of the land in Curridge belonged to the Church Commissioners and in the mid 19th century, just over an acre of land was bought by the Wasey family to build a 'school room and master's residence'. After their deaths the building and land were given to the Chieveley school board in 1886, with the proviso that the vicar and his successors should have 'exclusive use of the school building for the whole of Sunday, Christmas Day, Good Friday and on every Wednesday and Friday evening after 5 o'clock'!

Continue past the school as the track narrows to a grassy path descending to an unmade road coming in from the right.

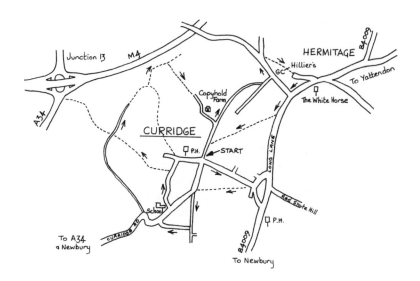

Keep straight on, passing a mixture of modern and older houses and cottages, including the old chapel, until you come to the Georgian house on the left, 200 yards from the chapel. Turn left here, notice the house name on the gate, and enter the field ahead by means of the stile. Cross this field to the next stile. There may be shire horses and Jacob sheep, owned by a retired farmer, in the adjacent fields. The new houses on the right are built on the site of the old brickworks.

Cross the stile and bear right to a stile leading into the woods. These woods are resplendent in spring with prim-roses, anemones and bluebells, and a picture to see. Climb up the slight hill and continue ahead, ignoring all paths to the right or left. On your right you will see sand extraction going on in the fields and for the time being the footpath is diverted round this work. A very pleasant tree-lined path has been created, although it is much closer to the M4. Continue round this clockwise until at the end of the diversion you see a natural gap in the hedge on the left where there was once a gate. Go through this and turn immediately right and follow the edge of the field with the hedge on your right-hand side. You will see evidence of sand extraction again through the hedge that has been carried out over the past few years. Follow

76

this around, with the motorway down to your left, until you cross a tarmac road and enter the small wood by a bridleway sign. The path leads through the wood to join another coming in from the right. Keep left, and within a few yards, join the farm access road from the left. You are now at Copyhold Farm. Just past the barn on the left, and the stables on the right, turn sharp left down a tree-lined road. Look out for geese and peacocks at the farm. Continue to the next junction and bear left here.

Walk along the track with woodland on your right, eventually passing through the Army Camp environs, with their community centre on the right and main gate on the left. Here you meet the road opposite Hillier's Garden Centre. Cross the road and turn left. Walk along the road verge to the end of the garden centre grounds, where there is a road signposted to Oare. Turn right, and within a few yards, turn right again, down a grassy path marked with a footpath sign, and continue along here for about ½ mile until you reach a lane with bungalows on the right, and then on, until you meet the main road.

Turn right here, and pass The White Horse public house and a garage on the left. At the crossroads (within 200 yards) go straight across, but keep to the right-hand side.

Just past the last house, as you meet the wood, is a footpath sign pointing into the wood. Because of storm damage it is easier to continue along the road a little further (to just before the Hermitage village sign), and you will see a clear path leading into the wood. Having walked through some dense bushes, you will soon meet a clearly defined path crossing the one you are on. Turn left and continue on, passing some houses on your right. Keep straight on, over three crossways until you emerge on a wide track with power lines running the whole length. Turn right here, and you will find yourself in Crab Tree Lane, only 200 yards from where you started.

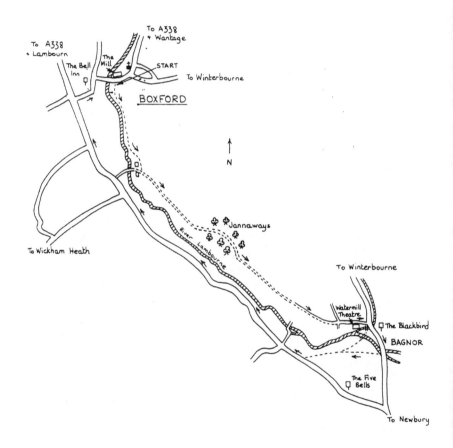

20
BOXFORD AND
THE RIVER LAMBOURN

★ INTRODUCTION: The Lambourn valley in west Berkshire is an area of outstanding natural beauty and this exhilarating walk follows the river Lambourn on part of the Lambourn Valley Way, a long distance walk from the Ridgeway at White Horse Hill in Oxfordshire to the Kennet and Avon canal towpath in Newbury. The walk begins in the village of Boxford, a photographer's delight with its thatched cottages and well kept gardens.

Boxford's history goes back many centuries. Roman and Saxon remains have been found in the area and Boxford Mill, where the walk begins, was mentioned in the Domesday Book. The mill stopped operating as such in the 1920s and is now a private house, with a picturesque garden. There are a number of delightful thatched cottages, and the nearby church of St Andrew dates back to Norman times. A pleasant hour could easily be spent here looking around before or after the walk along the Lambourn.

★ DISTANCE: 6 miles.

★ REFRESHMENTS: Available in the village of Boxford at the Bell Inn (½ mile from the start of the walk at Boxford Mill), and The Blackbird at Bagnor village. The Watermill Theatre also advertises a bar and buffet lunch.

★ HOW TO GET THERE: From Newbury take the valley road towards Lambourn for 4 miles to the Bell Inn at Boxford.

Turn right through the village, bearing first left then right over the bridge to the Mill House on the left.

★ THE WALK: Leave Boxford Mill and take the marked public footpath opposite, over unspoilt meadows where wild flowers abound, following the river Lambourn, a fast flowing trout stream. Within ¾ mile the path takes you behind old farm buildings and there is a private track leading right, over a small bridge to the Lambourn road, a pleasant place to stop and look for wildlife on the river.

After another ¾ mile, with water-meadows on your right and arable land to the left, you reach Jannaways, a small wood of mixed trees. Take the path which goes through the wood, where the sunlight filters through to wild flowers – honeysuckle, campanula, bluebells and wild violets in their season.

At the end of the wood, ignore the path to the left and continue on the main path, with a hedge on the left and a post and rail fence on the right. There is a good view of the hamlet of Woodspeen in the valley to the right.

At the end of this path, at a T-junction, turn left onto a track which becomes a lane and goes through part of the grounds of Bagnor Manor. After passing the main gate into the Manor on the right, the lane passes the Watermill Theatre. This was a working mill, but is now a popular professional theatre in a most beautiful setting. Turning right, onto the road to Newbury, you go through the small village of Bagnor. The Blackbird Inn is a good place to pause for refreshment.

Leaving the inn on the left, continue on the road for a few hundred yards over the river bridge. Take the public footpath to the right immediately after crossing the bridge. The river is on the right, but hidden by a timber fence and trees. The field alongside the path is planted with Norway Spruce. Follow the footpath/bridleway notices until you reach the road to Lambourn. Turn right and continue to Boxford, turn right again, and this brings you back to the mill.

21
UPPER BASILDON
─────────────────★─────────────────

★ INTRODUCTION: An exhilarating walk at the edge of the Berkshire Downs over gently rolling hills, with attractive vistas of fields and woods, and the occasional cluster of cottages or farm buildings.

Upper Basildon is about 3 miles west of Pangbourne and the village is surrounded by fields and woods crisscrossed by footpaths, byways and bridleways.

St Stephen's church was built in the 1960s beside the vicarage, on land which was once the vicar's orchard. Some older residents remember scrumping apples there. The Beehive Inn used to provide shelter for drovers taking sheep to market in Reading, although it has been much enlarged in recent years.

★ DISTANCE: About 5 miles. The walk is suitable for dogs and they do not have to be kept on the lead for much of the time. This walk involves some hills, giving you a good excuse to rest a moment and really soak in the beauty of your surroundings.

★ REFRESHMENTS: The Beehive Inn and The Red Lion are close by at the end of the walk, and although the Beehive is now a restaurant, it does provide bar lunches.

★ HOW TO GET THERE: Pangbourne, 7 miles west of Reading, lies on the junction of the A329 (Reading to Oxford) and the A340 from Theale. From the Reading direction, turn left at the mini roundabout opposite The Copper Inn, and take the first right turn between the church and a row of black and white cottages. After about a mile take the right fork towards Aldworth, and a further 2 miles brings you to Upper Basildon, with St Stephen's church to the right at one corner of the

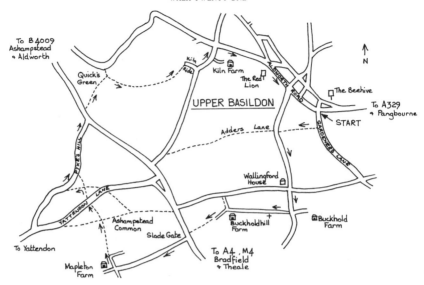

triangular village green. The walk starts and finishes at the church, where there is car parking space.

★ THE WALK: The walk starts from Gardeners Lane, at the corner of the village green opposite The Beehive. On the left some of the older cottages have been enlarged but the name Witneys has been kept. Turn right at the side of 4 Witneys, following the byway known as Adders Lane. At the end of the lane, turn left onto the metalled road to the crossroads. At the right of the crossroads is Wallingford House, known locally as The Coffee House. Legend has it that in this house two sisters set up a meeting place for those who did not want to patronise the local inns.

Go straight across the crossroads, signposted Bradfield and Theale. This is the hamlet of Buckhold, and at the next crossroads Buckhold Grange and Buckhold Farm are just visible to the left through a gap in the hedge. The road ahead is known to some as Suicide Lane, due to the inappropriate speeds some drivers use in this very narrow road. Turn right and walk towards Buckhold church, now a private house.

Walk beside a magnificent line of copper beeches, past the Pick Your Own Fruit fields and farm buildings. The antique pump and horse trough with decorative feet are worth noting, still used for their original purpose and not as ornate flower baskets. On the left are tiny cottages (using the same numbering system as those by the church), and ahead a footpath beckons towards the woods.

The path leads straight ahead and as it descends the view of the valley opens up. Go through a fixed kissing gate to Slade Gate (a dry valley); holly, hornbeam, oak, maple, hazel, beech and spindle add varied greens to the landscape. At the bottom of the hill, the path goes between two old cottages.

Turn left, then almost immediately right, up the road sign-posted to Mapletons and Strouds, the road gradually sloping upwards. The hedgerows are a delight with poppies, pale pink and white bindweed, ragwort and scabious – look backwards to enjoy the flowers in the foreground and the wooded hills in the distance. Beech has been planted to form a new hedge on the left, and beyond this the field is some-times aglow with the brilliant yellow of rape.

At Mapletons Farm take the footpath on the right, gently descending to the foot of a hill field. This bit can be very muddy in wet weather. Cross another footpath and go straight ahead across the field which stretches along the hillside, towards a wooden gate leading into the deliciously cool woods of Ashampstead Common, just the choice on a hot day, or shelter on a cold one.

Cross the Yattendon road and take the path directly opposite, and at a T-junction footpath in the middle of the woods, turn left. The path reaches Pykes Hill Road; to the left there is an attractive group of cottages.

Turn right onto Pykes Hill Road. The views as you walk down the road are of rolling hills, skyline trees. A 'vertical' hedge on the opposite hill, beyond the houses in the valley, indicates our path climbing the hill.

At the road junction turn left, passing the attractive old Pyt Cottages. An old VR postbox set into the cottage wall is marked 'no longer in use', superseded by a metal box on a post at the road junction. Cross the road to take the footpath on the right – an iron railing helps the traveller to climb easily.

The views on all sides are well worth a slow climb up the hill path, with pauses for admiring glances as well as regaining one's breath – truly England's green and pleasant land.

A slip gate leads you to an old Methodist chapel (dated 1872) at Quicks Green. Turn right onto a path which dips into a wooded dell, the valley coming into view on your right.

Over a high stile, the path crosses the field. Turn right and pass between the large modern house on the right and a small estate of houses called Kiln Ride. Turn right into Kiln Ride, and pass two older houses which still retain the old name of Kiln Bolton. At the road junction turn left up the hill, passing on the right a large house, Kiln Bolton House, which is on the site of two cottages which were also part of the Kiln Bolton row of cottages. A little further on on the right is Kiln Farm, parts of which date back to the 17th century.

The large building on the left at the crossroads is the local Scout HQ. At the crossroads turn right towards Pangbourne, with another lovely view of fields and woods to the right as you descend the hill.

Take care at the next crossroads, cars tend to hurtle downhill and the view is somewhat obscured. Turn right along the main road towards Pangbourne, where at the next crossroads The Red Lion offers the chance of refreshment. Passing (or leaving) The Red Lion, continue up the hill in the Pangbourne direction to reach the village green and St Stephen's.

22
A DOWNS WALK
AROUND ALDWORTH

★ INTRODUCTION: This exhilarating yet easy walk is over open downland near the Ridgeway, giving extensive views over to Oxfordshire. Along the way the route passes woodlands which are filled with bluebells in springtime.

Aldworth is an unspoilt Berkshire village owing its origins to the Ridgeway, one of the most ancient highways in Britain. It was once a centre for sheep farming, enjoying a close proximity to East Ilsley and Compton and their sheep fairs.

★ DISTANCE: 4 country miles!

★ REFRESHMENTS: The Bell Inn, in the same family for 200 years, is in the centre of the village, and has been the CAMRA's 'Pub of the Year' on several occasions.

★ HOW TO GET THERE: The walk starts at Aldworth church, which is approximately 9 miles north-north east of Newbury, on the B4009 to Streatley.

★ THE WALK: This is a very good Downland walk for a fine day. Start at Aldworth church, where 120 yards downhill from the lower church gate, a path marked 'bridleway' leads off to the right, just past a white cottage.

Continue along this path until you reach the road. Here turn right, and immediately turn right again towards Pibworth Farm, following the public footpath sign.

At the farmhouse gate turn right, across a plank bridge following the footpath sign, before you get into the farm

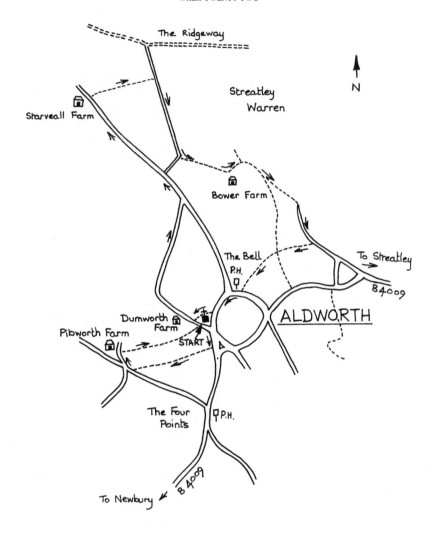

yard Keep close to the fence on the right. Cross the stile and continue through three fields, over four more stiles, keeping to the left hand fence, until you almost come back to the church

At this farm lane turn left past Dunworth Farm going towards open downland. Head uphill, towards the crest of

86

the hill, igoring the grassy track to the left. Just over the crest, turn left along a metalled road to Starveall Farm, passing Warren Farm on the right. There are wonderful views ahead into Oxfordshire and of the villages of East Ilsley and Compton nestling in the hollows. Just imagine how isolated Starveall Farm was a few decades ago. (The Warren used to provide food for shepherds who took their flocks to Starveall in summer. Starveall farms are common in sheep country, suggesting that in these high up places, there was little to feed man or beast.)

Opposite the farmhouse turn right at the footpath sign, with the large barn on your left, and keep close to the right-hand fence heading towards the high ground. Look back over those views!

As you start to descend, Streatley and the Thames valley come into view. As the path meets a farm track, over to the left you may see the Ridgeway footpath, but here we turn right and follow the track for approximately ½ mile to where the track turns sharp right. On this corner there is a metal gate on the left, with Bower Farm beyond. This part of the footpath is unmarked. Go through the gate, up the bank on the right to the fence, and follow this fence all the way to the farm gate. Don't go through the farm gate, but keep in this field and head towards a metal gate on the far side of the field.

Through this gate you meet a grassy track. Head over the hill to the right and follow this path for about ¾ mile, until it joins another track coming in from the left. Bear right here and continue until you see a footpath sign on the right. This heads back to the village of Aldworth across two fields, ending in a narrow path between the cricket field and the Bell Inn garden. Cross the road to the village well, and then follow the road back to the church, passing between the old school, the village shop and the post office.

23

LAMBOURN

---★---

★ INTRODUCTION: The town of Lambourn, at the foot of the Lambourn Downs, provides the focal point for this exhilarating walk over open countryside, with magnificent views and a wealth of wild flowers and trees to be enjoyed.

Lambourn's history goes back many centuries, to Roman times, and its prosperity once depended upon the sheep which grazed the open chalk downland surrounding the town. Two sheep fairs a year were being held by the 13th century. The town lies in the Lambourn valley, the river Lambourn rising nearby.

Lambourn's connection with racing began in the 18th century, when the Earl of Craven was responsible for encouraging race meetings at nearby Ashdown park. Today some of the racing world's top trainers are to be found in the area and the town's livelihood is closely bound up with the fortunes of the flat and national hunt. The lychgate of St Michael and All Angels is itself a memorial to a Victorian racehorse trainer, William Jousiffe.

★ DISTANCE: About 5 miles.

★ REFRESHMENTS: There are no refreshments on the walk itself, but several places within Lambourn on your return.

★ HOW TO GET THERE: Lambourn lies on the B4000 from Newbury. Park in the car park in the High Street.

★ THE WALK: From the car park, re-enter the High Street, turning right and walking south-east to the end of the street. Turn left and go along Edwards Hill. After about 100 yards turn

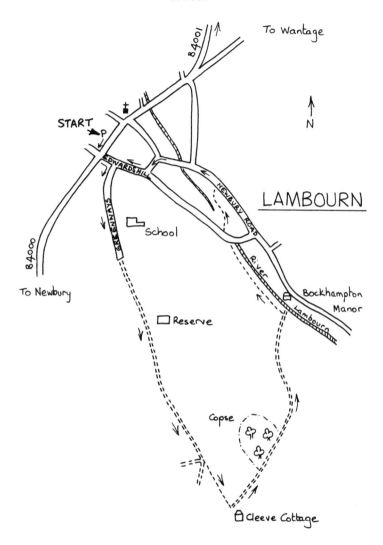

right into Greenways and continue up a slight gradient. The tarmac road then becomes a gravel bridleway. The Lambourn primary school is on your left.

You are now on the ancient Lambourn to Hungerford road, and in the spring and summer there is a wide variety of wild flowers to be seen. Keep to the left whenever the bridleway divides.

On your left you will pass the Watts Reserve, a grassland reserve belonging to the Berks, Bucks and Oxfordshire Naturalists Trust (BBONT). A notice at the first stile summarises its interest and it is open to visitors.

The walk meanders along this attractive path, with high hedges and trees on either side. Turn sharp left at Cleeve Cottage, a 15th century thatched cottage. Opposite, at the site of a former well, stands a pollarded example of our only native maple, the field maple. Its girth is considerable for the species. The path now continues north-east, still with hedges and trees on either side and a good selection of wild flowers and shrubs to be enjoyed.

At the north-west corner of Cleeve Wood, the nearby 'Strawberry Field', part of the Cleeve Hill Site of Scientific Interest, may be visited on foot by prior arrangement with BBONT, who manage it on behalf of English Nature.

A short distance brings the walker to Thornhill Copse, a typical coppice woodland on a clay cap over chalk. The neglected hazel now grows leggily under oak and ash, with wild cherry and field maple also present. This is a fine bluebell and primrose wood. Turning north-west at the top of the hill there are magnificent views of Lambourn and turning north-east you can see Eastbury and East Garston.

Continue downhill to Bockhampton Manor. Just before the manor, turn left over a stile and walk alongside the river Lambourn (often dry). Notice on your right the small brick bridge denoting the route of the old Lambourn Valley Railway. Continue over two fields until a road is reached. Walk along the road for 150 yards and after passing a barn on your right leave the road to climb over a stile. Go over a small field, over another stile and skirt the side of the Lambourn Sports Field. The path then goes through a new housing estate. At the end turn right and continue along until you come to Newbury Road.

Turn left, walk along for about 150 yards and at Station Road turn left. Walk to the end and turn right. You are now at Edwards Hill. After 200 yards you rejoin the route of the initial part of the walk. Retrace your footsteps back to the car park.

24

HUNGERFORD

<hr>

★ INTRODUCTION: This enjoyable town and country walk is full of interest, combining Hungerford's historic town centre with the river Kennet, the canal, delightful scenery and hill views. A gradual climb takes the route out of the river valley to the village of Leverton, with its thatched cottages, before dropping back once again to Hungerford.

Hungerford is still a small market town, as it has been for centuries. In the 14th century John of Gaunt granted the inhabitants the right to fish, shoot and graze on the common and Freeman's Marsh. This was confirmed by Elizabeth I in 1574. These rights are still in operation and enjoyed by the present Commoners. Each year, after Easter, the Hocktide Court meets to elect officers for the ensuing year. There are many interesting buildings to be found in the town, and one of Hungerford's most familiar landmarks is the Bear Hotel; there has been a coaching inn on the site since the 13th century, though the present building is Georgian. The rivers Kennet and Dun, which are famous for their trout, run through the northern edge of the town.

★ DISTANCE: The walk is just under 4 miles in length.

★ REFRESHMENTS: There are many public houses in the town, and refreshments can also be obtained at the Tutti Pole near the canal bridge, Manthy's Pantry at the Railway Cuttings or the Antique Arcade, 50 yards past the Town Clock. 100 yards from the Town Clock, and on the opposite side of the street from the Antique Arcade, is The Tea Pot.

★ HOW TO GET THERE: Turn off the A4 in Hungerford into

the High Street (A338). There is Pay and Display parking in the town or limited free parking at St Lawrence's church. To reach the church from the High Street, turn into Church Street and walk along, passing the fire station, to take the first turning on the right. Carry on under the railway bridge, keeping left along the road, until you reach the arched gate which forms the entrance to the church.

★ THE WALK: The walk commences from the gate of St Lawrence's church. While you are here, note the unusual clapper stile into the churchyard and the Bath stone which was used to rebuild the church in 1816, when the new canal made this famous building stone available in Hungerford for the first time.

Walk through an avenue of trees past the nursery school, the Croft Hall and the town bowls and tennis club. Carry on through the alley to the High Street, over the zebra crossing, down the High Street and cross the bridge over the Kennet and Avon Canal. At the junction of Bridge Street and the A4, turn right, leaving The Bear on your left. Take care on the

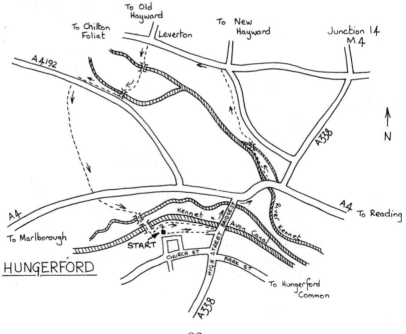

92

narrow footpath by the old fire station, now called 'The Fireplace'.

Walk on to the fine stone bridge over the river Kennet. At the centre of the bridge, cross the A4 with care, and continue to the end of the bridge, immediately turning left on to the path between the two rivers. Follow to the end of the path and cross the footbridge, then, diagonally take the signed path to walk along the top of the well-cultivated allotments.

At the end of the obvious path, cross the drive of the bungalow on the left and pick up the footpath again, not so well walked this time, along the edge of the cornfield. At the top of the path, join the road signposted Leverton and Chilton Foliat. At Leverton, turn left. Walk on, passing the quaint thatched cottages on your left, and on over the bridge over the river Kennet.

Keep to the footpath over the Hatches and river and go up the steps to the B4192. Turn right and walk about 200 yards until the footpath sign on the opposite bank, 'Hungerford 1.5 miles', is reached. Cross the road with care. The footpath leads straight up across the field, but the crop is cut by the farmer to ease walking. Cross the stile at the top of the bank (steep step) and keep to the edge of the field to walk towards Hungerford, going south.

There are steps at the end of the path down on to the edge of the A4. Cross with care. Go left for a short distance until you come to a stile. Climb this and walk diagonally left to the bottom of the field. At the bottom, cross the bridge, veer left, following the footpath, and then cross the footbridge.

You have come almost full circle. Cross the swingbridge over the canal, turn left and carry on along the towpath until you see the canal bridge in front, then turn right into the High Street.

25
INKPEN

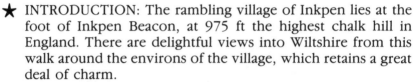

★ INTRODUCTION: The rambling village of Inkpen lies at the foot of Inkpen Beacon, at 975 ft the highest chalk hill in England. There are delightful views into Wiltshire from this walk around the environs of the village, which retains a great deal of charm.

Inkpen's unusual name is derived from the 'pen' or enclosure of the Saxon chief Inga, and indicates the village's ancient origins. The beacon and the downs obviously dominate the village, and many people visit the area to see the famous gibbet on the hill – not the original, which was first erected in 1676.

Pottery Lane was named from the local pottery industry, which closed in the early 1900s. It was well known for its robust pottery, used for articles such as bread crocks, pitchers and cream jars, made from the yellow clay that gave the name 'Inkpen Yellow Legs' to the village labourers.

★ DISTANCE: 4½ miles.

★ REFRESHMENTS: There are none en route, but two public houses in the village.

★ HOW TO GET THERE: Inkpen lies approximately 3 miles south-east of Hungerford, and 2 miles east of the A338. At the south end of Hungerford High Street turn left into Priory Road, and take the fourth turning left, Inkpen Road, just beyond the Priory. Follow this road to Inkpen. Park at the recreation ground, near the post office.

★ THE WALK: Follow the concrete road (Pottery Lane) on the

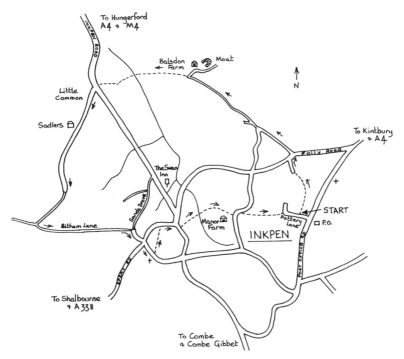

south-west side of the recreation ground, and turn right through a gap in the hedge, before the first house on the left. Skirt the playing fields, following the hedge to a second gap. Bear slightly left, crossing a track, and take the sandy path which winds through the scrub to the open area at Robins Hill. Continue along the left of the garages and down the road to Folly Road. Turn right and, very shortly afterwards, left on to a gravel track before the first house on the left. Proceed straight along this track through the wood; then with a field on the right and a copse on the left. This track becomes a concrete strip leading to Balsdon Farm, where the remains of an old moat can still be seen.

There is a sharp right-hand bend in the track just before the farm buildings: go left through the gateway and follow the bridlepath sign, taking an easily distinguished path across the field to some conifers. Continue through this woodland and, at the stream, go through the gate into the field. Bear a little left, crossing the field, and proceed uphill to another gate,

95

and more woodland. Take the path through the scrubland, bearing to the right where the path seems to divide, and reach the Inkpen-Hungerford road. Take a left-right 'dog-leg' to a small road signposted 'Sadlers'. This area is Little Common. Continue along the road for ¾ mile, and onwards up a track where the road ends. At the T-junction, turn left into Bitham Lane, which follows the line of the ridge between Shalbourne and Inkpen, and was once a drovers' road. Keep the chalk pit on the left and continue downhill to the junction with Sands Drove. Bear right along this track to reach the Inkpen-Ham road.

Cross over, and walk up to the old rectory and St Michael's church, built on a knoll. Although restored in 1896, the church dates back to Norman times. The oak lychgate was made at the local sawmills (now closed), by craftsmen in the parish in memory of a Rector, Henry Dobree Butler, who died in 1935, the last of a family of Butlers who had held office in the church since 1700. The rectory is a fine example of 17th century architecture, and there is also a tithe barn to be seen. There are delightful views of Wiltshire from this point.

There is a signposted footpath almost opposite that leading up to the church. Take this across the field towards the left-hand side of West Court House. Turn right at the road, and continue to the junction with the road to Combe. A little further on, turn on to a footpath between two cottages. Climb over the stile, cross the field and then the bridge. Proceed uphill, keeping the fence on your left. Cross another stile into the field, continue until a further stile is reached. Cross this and turn right between fences, and at the farm buildings turn left over another stile. Continue alongside the fence, keeping it on your right, following it as it turns sharp right and, at the farm road continue straight on. Where the road bends sharply to the left, continue across the field ahead, aiming for a large oak tree.

Here there is another stile; cross this and follow the fence uphill to a laurel bush. Keeping to the right of the bush, cross the stile into Pottery Lane. This was named from the pottery kiln, which closed early in the 1900s. Turn right, and walk along Pottery Lane back to the starting point.